Andreas Freitag

A Controlling Model for the Enterprise Architecture and SOA

Andreas Freitag

A Controlling Model for the Enterprise Architecture and SOA

Increased Cost Transparency for Modular IT Architectures

VDM Verlag Dr. Müller

Imprint

Bibliographic information by the German National Library: The German National Library lists this publication at the German National Bibliography; detailed bibliographic information is available on the Internet at http://dnb.d-nb.de.
   Any brand names and product names mentioned in this book are subject to trademark, brand or patent protection and are trademarks or registered trademarks of their respective holders. The use of brand names, product names, common names, trade names, product descriptions etc. even without a particular marking in this works is in no way to be construed to mean that such names may be regarded as unrestricted in respect of trademark and brand protection legislation and could thus be used by anyone.

Cover image: www.purestockx.com

Publisher:
VDM Verlag Dr. Müller Aktiengesellschaft & Co. KG, Dudweiler Landstr. 125 a, 66123 Saarbrücken, Germany,
Phone +49 681 9100-698, Fax +49 681 9100-988,
Email: info@vdm-verlag.de

Copyright © 2008 VDM Verlag Dr. Müller Aktiengesellschaft & Co. KG and licensors
All rights reserved. Saarbrücken 2008

Produced in USA and UK by:
Lightning Source Inc., La Vergne, Tennessee, USA
Lightning Source UK Ltd., Milton Keynes, UK
BookSurge LLC, 5341 Dorchester Road, Suite 16, North Charleston, SC 29418, USA

ISBN: 978-3-8364-8519-7

Preface

While the importance of IT to support or even enable modern business models increases, the strategic imperative for the CIO is shifting from "do more with less" towards "make the difference". According to the well-known statement of Michael E. Porter, companies can differentiate themselves from their competitors by delivering higher value to customers or by creating a comparable value at lower cost, or by doing both. In order to identify potentials for generating an improved competitive position on a company level, knowing the underlying cost structures thoroughly is indispensable. However, the majority of customer organizations we gained insight into during our projects only know their IT costs from a financial management perspective.

In most cases, IT budgets are allocated according to historically established cost centre structures using a set of allocation keys or pricing mechanisms. These cost data structures do not match to the granularity of modern Enterprise Architectures. Consequently, many companies struggle to determine the real profit margin of their products based on a marketable price while taking into account all relevant costs – starting from IT infrastructure over applications and databases to processes. Therefore, the CIO's mission of differentiated, value-oriented IT management can only be successful with an adequate approach to increase target-oriented IT cost transparency. Back to Porter's statement: how does a company make the difference without knowing the real costs of their products?

This is just one example and it was only one motivation for us to entrust Andreas Freitag with the development of a novel controlling model for IT architectures. In this book, he describes the controlling model and different common scenarios where the traditional way of assessing IT costs may not lead to an optimal solution on the company level.

The model described in this book was proven during a complex Enterprise Architecture project with the goal to develop an overarching CRM strategy and IT roadmap for a large international group. It was the basis for a more precise business case delivering improved information to decide about the migration strategy from monolithic legacy IT architectures towards a modern SOA-solution environment.

I am sure that the controlling model described in this book will gain increased importance with a growing maturity level and adoption of Service-oriented Architectures. Management members and IT architects who have to decide about spending related to IT will find new impulses for their daily work and an approach which can be tailored to their own situation.

Bonn, March 2008

Uwe Weber
Managing Partner
Detecon International GmbH

Acknowledgement

This book is based on the results of a study conducted for the group "Architecture Strategy" of Detecon International GmbH. In the meantime, the practical relevance of the developed controlling model has been proven by its successful application in several consulting projects. Hence, I became passionate about this topic and it is still subject to my ongoing research.

I would like to take the opportunity of this publication to express my gratitude to those people who accompanied me on my way and thus contributed to this publication:

- Detecon's Architecture Strategy team - especially Dr. Verena Schmidtmann and Uwe Weber - for offering their expertise, sharing their practical experiences and many valuable ideas and suggestions. They enabled me to work on my favorite topic and provided their help and guidance in research.
- My good friends Dirk Herrmann and the Furrer brothers for looking closely at my English style and grammar, correcting both and offering suggestions for continual improvement.
- Maria for excellent working conditions, first of all spoiling me with her culinary skills every day.

I would like to give my special thanks to my family for constantly supporting me in my personal and professional development and, in particular, to my beloved wife Eva for enjoying all the really important things in life with me.

Bonn, March 2008   Andreas Freitag
                                                                   Consultant
                                                       Detecon International GmbH

Table of contents

1	**Introduction**	**15**
1.1	Motivation	15
1.2	Goal	15
1.3	Structure	16
1.4	Practical relevance and applicability	17
2	**Description of the architectural environment**	**18**
2.1	Enterprise Architecture	18
	2.1.1 Introduction to Enterprise Architecture	18
	2.1.2 The Zachman Framework	22
	2.1.3 The Open Group Architecture Framework (TOGAF)	24
2.2	Service Oriented Architecture	27
	2.2.1 Introduction to SOA	27
	2.2.2 Definition of service orientation	29
	2.2.3 Benefits of SOA	31
	2.2.4 Potential cost savings through SOA	38
2.3	Enterprise Architecture and SOA	39
3	**IT controlling**	**42**
3.1	Introduction to controlling	42
3.2	IT controlling	43
	3.2.1 Structure of IT controlling	43
	3.2.2 IT supply side: controlling IT service provision	44
	3.2.3 IT demand side: controlling IT service usage	45
	3.2.4 IT governance	46
3.3	Operative versus strategic controlling	47
3.4	Strategic IT controlling	48
3.5	Special requirements for the given architectural environment	48
4	**Controlling model development**	**50**
4.1	How to derive the controlling model	50
	4.1.1 Definition of purposes	50
	4.1.2 Basic principles	50
	4.1.3 Cost accounting basics	51
	4.1.4 Definition of objectives	52
4.2	The building block approach	53
	4.2.1 TOGAF's building block definition	53

	4.2.2	Decoupling of logical and physical architecture 54
	4.2.3	Enterprise Architecture Management with building blocks 55
	4.2.4	Building block ownership 56
	4.2.5	Granularity of financial analyses 57
4.3	The SOA layer model 58
	4.3.1	Detecon's SOA layer model 58
	4.3.2	Building blocks in the SOA layer model 60
	4.3.3	Controlling the SOA layer model 62
	4.3.4	Characterization of business processes 64
4.4	Determination of building block costs 65
	4.4.1	Initial considerations 65
	4.4.2	Detecon's Business Enabling Approach 65
	4.4.3	Capital Expenditures versus Operational Expenditures 67
	4.4.4	Building block budgeting 67
	4.4.5	IT value map 69
	4.4.6	The cost element matrix 71
	4.4.7	Implications for controlling 73
4.5	Pricing of building block services 73
4.6	Pricing of business services and infrastructure services 75
	4.6.1	The concept of virtual services 75
	4.6.2	Using virtual services for controlling 76
4.7	Controlling IT demand 77
	4.7.1	Planning costs and cost allocation 77
	4.7.2	Service usage planning and enterprise-internal marketing 78
	4.7.3	Business service pricing 78
4.8	Controlling model overview 80
	4.8.1	Summarizing the model 80
	4.8.2	Calculation example 81
4.9	Controlling maturity model 83
5	**Controlling model application** **85**
5.1	IT supply side 85
5.2	IT demand side 86
5.3	Sourcing decisions and legacy system valuation 88
	5.3.1	Outsourcing 88
	5.3.2	Visualizing sourcing objects in the SOA layer model 90
	5.3.3	Building block sourcing 91
	5.3.4	Business Process (Out-)sourcing (BPO) 92
	5.3.5	Legacy system valuation 93

	5.3.6 Summarizing sourcing calculation support	94
6	**Conclusion**	**96**
6.1	Summary	96
6.2	Model applicability	97
6.3	Recommendations for further research	98

Appendix A: SOA layer model – UML class diagram **100**

Bibliography **101**

List of figures

Figure 1: The Zachman Framework 22
Figure 2: TOGAF ADM basic structure 25
Figure 3: TOGAF Enterprise Continuum 26
Figure 4: SOA fosters business agility 33
Figure 5: Enterprise Architecture Management for SOA 41
Figure 6: Structure of IT controlling 44
Figure 7: Logical decoupling and building block-internal layers 54
Figure 8: A scalable system of planning objects 55
Figure 9: Concepts for Building Block Management 56
Figure 10: Granularity of financial analyses 57
Figure 11: Detecon's SOA layer model 59
Figure 12: Information model for Enterprise Architecture Management ... 59
Figure 13: Detailed view on an ABB in the application layer 61
Figure 14: Detailed view on an ABB in the infrastructure layer 61
Figure 15: Controlling the SOA layer model 63
Figure 16: Detecon's Business Enabling Approach 66
Figure 17: Building block budgeting 68
Figure 18: IT value map 70
Figure 19: Cost element matrix 72
Figure 20: Business service - planning, costing, pricing 77
Figure 21: Defining IT service prices 79
Figure 22: Controlling model overview 81
Figure 23: Calculation example 82
Figure 24: Controlling maturity model 83
Figure 25: Controlling maturity visualized 84
Figure 26: Enabling controlling of IT supply 85
Figure 27: Enabling Activity Based Costing 86
Figure 28: Possible sourcing objects 91
Figure 29: Legacy system valuation 93
Figure 30: Information aggregation and decomposition 94

List of abbreviations

ABB	Architecture Building Block
ABC	Activity Based Costing
ADM	Architecture Development Method
ASP	Application Service Provider
B2B	Business to Business
BI	Business Intelligence
BPO	Business Process Outsourcing
CAPEX	Capital Expenditures
CIO	Chief Information Officer
CTO	Chief Technology Officer
CRM	Customer Relationship Management
EA	Enterprise Architecture
EAI	Enterprise Application Integration
EAM	Enterprise Architecture Management
EPC	Event-driven Process Chain
ERP	Enterprise Resource Planning
ESA	Enterprise Services Architecture
HR	Human Resources
IGC	International Group of Controlling
ITGI	IT Governance Institute
LOB	Line of Business
OECD	Organization for Economic Cooperation and Development
OPEX	Operational Expenditures
ROI	Return on Investment
SBB	Solution Building Block
SCM	Supply Chain Management
SIB	TOGAF Standards Information Base
SLA	Service Level Agreement
SOA	Service Oriented Architecture
TCO	Total Cost of Ownership
TOGAF	The Open Group Architecture Framework
TRM	TOGAF Technical Reference Model
SCM	Supply Chain Management
ZIFA	Zachman Institute for Framework Advancement

1 Introduction

1.1 Motivation

Today, a company's IT is challenged to support new business processes in continuously shortening cycles and to adapt to company structure or business strategy changes in a flexible way. Simultaneously, it is exposed to cost pressures, which impedes a continual development or replacement of systems in a classical way. A flexible Enterprise Architecture promises to resolve this dilemma by modularization, layering, and enterprise-wide integration. Service Oriented Architecture (SOA) is a suitable possibility to implement the Enterprise Architecture. Modularization is achieved by definition and flexible connection of building blocks. The SOA layer model structures the enterprise's IT into functional layers. Enterprise-wide integration of building blocks realizes synergies such as reuse-benefits across different Lines of Business (LOB) and enables controlling on enterprise level. New business processes can be supported by (re-)composing existing building blocks, without generating costs of conventional software development projects. Thus the adoption of SOA increases IT flexibility and operational efficiency which leads to increased business agility. It enhances the capability to respond to market demands by fostering the successful support of new business processes. Thereby it promotes innovation and growth and it can lead to a sustainable competitive advantage.

To realize and measure the advantages mentioned above it is necessary to monitor and control the financial aspects. Since there is no matured controlling model for this kind of architecture, it is the goal of this book to develop a controlling model for the evaluation of building blocks and the services provided during their entire lifecycle.

1.2 Goal

Regarding the combination of financial controlling issues, Enterprise Architecture and SOA, research can be conducted concerning two different issues:

First, any investment in IT infrastructure has to be made plausible to non-technical stakeholders, like top management, by providing predictable and verifiable returns. An investment in SOA increases process efficiency and decreases future investments, but many of today's controlling systems are not able to attribute them to the infrastructure.[1] Thus, investment valuation methods have to be analyzed regarding their applicability for SOA. There are already publications available about measuring the value of Enterprise Architecture and SOA. Different approaches aim to proof the economic advantages of investments in architecture. In fact, most books on Enterprise Architecture and SOA include an economic motivation.

Second, after the decision to implement an Enterprise Architecture through SOA has been made, economic operation and strategic controlling has to be ensured. The focus of this book is to develop a controlling model for the given architectural environment, which ensures consistent cost determination and cost allocation, in order to allow for consistent financial calculations to support Enterprise Architecture Management.

1.3 Structure

In the second chapter, Enterprise Architecture and SOA are introduced to build a consistent information base. It will be shown that both concepts are complementary and have to be used in conjunction to reach the goal of increased IT flexibility and business agility.

The third chapter introduces IT controlling and the idea of differentiating IT supply and IT demand. After motivating improved cost transparency and the promotion of cost awareness, the chapter shows the special requirements emerging from the given architectural environment.

Chapter four is the main part of this work. After introducing the building block concept, the hierarchical order of planning objects in the Enterprise Architecture and the SOA layer model, it is shown how building block costs can be determined. Adjacently, a policy-based method for cost allocation is developed. At the end, a calculation example and a controlling maturity model are given.

Chapter five shows that the cost information gained can be used to support sourcing

---

[1] cf. Krafzig/Banke/Slama: Enterprise SOA 2005, p. 259

decisions and the examination of legacy systems.

Chapter six concludes this work by summarizing and generalizing findings of conducted research and benefits of applying the controlling model. Additionally, recommendations for further research are given.

1.4 Practical relevance and applicability

This study has been conducted in cooperation with the group Architecture Strategy of
> Detecon International GmbH
> Oberkasseler Straße 2
> 53227 Bonn
> www.detecon.de
> (in the following Detecon).

Therefore, the development of the controlling model is based on the Enterprise Architecture Management methods and structures applied by Detecon. This is not a drawback, because most of the methods and structures are valid universally. To ensure practical applicability and academic quality, each concept or model is validated by giving a reference to corresponding literature. Additionally, the controlling model is kept general where applicable.

2 Description of the architectural environment

2.1 Enterprise Architecture

2.1.1 Introduction to Enterprise Architecture

This first subchapter gives a set of definitions to build a consistent base for further description and analyses. The terms *'enterprise'*, *'architecture'*, *'Enterprise Architecture'* and *'Enterprise Architecture Framework'* are defined, as they are understood in this book. Additionally, two representative Enterprise Architecture Frameworks are presented: The Zachman Framework, as the 'father' of Enterprise Architecture Frameworks, and The Open Group Architecture Framework (TOGAF), as the one relevant for the research conducted in this work. All information given in the following chapters - unless quoted otherwise - has been gathered from The Open Group[2] or The Zachman Institute for Framework Advancement (ZIFA)[3] website.

A widely accepted definition for the term *'enterprise'* is

> *"Any collection of organizations that has a common set of goals or a single bottom line."*[4]

This definition is consistent with the existence of several independent lines of business forming an enterprise, where a *'Line of Business'* (LOB) is understood as

> *"A distinct area of activity within the enterprise. It may involve the manufacture of certain products, the provision of services, or internal administrative functions."*[5]

In literature, a large variety of differing definitions of *'architecture'* can be found.[6] The most apparent difference is that some definitions focus on the physical object itself, whereas others define architecture as the description of a physical object. While most

---

[2] cf. The Open Group: TOGAF website 2006
[3] cf. Zachman Institute for Framework Advancement: website 2006
[4] cf. Lankhorst et al.: Enterprise Architecture 2005, p. 3
[5] cf. Bernard: Enterprise Architecture 2005, p. 39
[6] As a matter of course, research was limited to IT-related business and economics literature.

authors decide for one of both possibilities, TOGAF deals with various definitions by accepting, that the term *'architecture'* has these two differing meanings, depending on the contextual usage:

> *"The structure of components, their interrelationships, and the principles and guidelines governing their design and evolution over time."*

or

> *"A formal description of a system, or a detailed plan of the system at component level to guide its implementation."*[7]

The first TOGAF definition is consistent with the conceptual definition of *'architecture'*, given by ANSI/IEEE Standard 1471-2000[8]:

> *"The fundamental organization of a system embodied in its components, their relationships to each other, and to the environment, and the principles guiding its design and evolution."*[9]

The architecture is represented in architectural descriptions, representing the viewpoint of each stakeholder. This is pointed out in the second definition. In this way, TOGAF tries to find a trade-off between applying the terminology commonly accepted by its user community and ensuring consistency to the concepts and terminology of ANSI/IEEE Standard 1471-2000[10], knowing that there are small inconsistencies. However, as the scope of this work is not a detailed discussion of terminology, they can be left unattended, as they do not cause problems. In the following, the TOGAF definitions given are applied in this book.

Consequently, *'Enterprise Architecture'* is an architecture for the entire enterprise. Again, literature is offering a large variety of definitions. The most applicable definition for *'Enterprise Architecture'* found is:

---

[7] cf. The Open Group: TOGAF FAQ 2002
[8] ANSI/IEEE Std 1471-2000 "IEEE Recommended Practice for Architectural Description of Software-Intensive Systems" was developed by the IEEE Architecture Working Group with representation from industry.
[9] cf. Institute of Electrical and Electronics Engineers: ANSI/IEEE Std 1471-2000 2000, p. 3
[10] A discussion on TOGAF's terminology can be found on the TOGAF website:
http://www.opengroup.org/architecture/togaf8-doc/arch/p4/views/vus_intro.htm#Terminology

> *"A coherent whole of principles, methods and models that are used in the design and realization of an enterprise's organizational structure, business processes, information systems and infrastructure."*[11]

For this work, as the most important fact, the Enterprise Architecture provides a holistic view on the enterprise, covering both business and IT domain, and ensuring alignment of business and organizational design of the enterprise with the IT architecture.

An *'Enterprise Architecture Framework'*

> *"... provides a structure for the Enterprise Architecture, by identifying and relating different architectural viewpoints and the corresponding modeling technique ... ",*[12]

leading to a complete and consistent description for analyzing the information about an organization and to enable the building of information systems that efficiently support the business.[13] In the following paragraphs, two representative Enterprise Architecture Frameworks are described.

The Zachman Framework, introduced in 1987 by the IBM researcher John A. Zachman as *"A framework for information systems architecture"*[14], was the first Enterprise Architecture Framework. In his paper, Zachman refers to principles of classical architecture and applies them to his framework for information systems. Since then, it has been constantly extended, refined and elaborated.[15] Recently, it was published as a 3D model on the ZIFA website. The Zachman Framework is method neutral, focusing on content.

The first TOGAF specification "TOGAF Version 1", published in 1995, was a generic framework and methodology for development of technical architectures. The latest version TOGAF 8.1 was published in 2004 and is labeled "The Enterprise Edition", pointing out to be a framework dedicated to Enterprise Architecture. It has been

---

[11] cf. Lankhorst et al.: Enterprise Architecture 2005, p. 3
[12] cf. Lankhorst et al.: Enterprise Architecture 2005, p. 20
[13] cf. Harrison/Varveris: Establishing TOGAF 2004, p. 1
[14] cf. Zachman: Framework for Information Systems Architecture 1987
[15] cf. Zachman: Extending the Framework 1992

continuously developed by members of The Open Group's Architecture Forum, which consists of representatives of IT customer and vendor organizations. TOGAF is an open and highly customizable framework, allowing for adaptation to a company's particular needs. Specification and documentation are freely available for any organization to develop an Enterprise Architecture for use within that organization.

Unlike the Zachman Framework, TOGAF contains a detailed method and a given set of supporting tools for developing an Enterprise Architecture.[16] Furthermore, it offers a common vocabulary, a list of recommended standards, and compliant products that can be used. Both Enterprise Architecture Frameworks address the complexity of today's information systems. Zachman's goal is to achieve holistic view on the enterprise, linking the different architectural views. The complete and consistent documentation of the Enterprise Architecture, should be comprehensible to everyone involved. The framework works as a communications device and facilitates architectural changes.[17] The emphasis of TOGAF lies on the initial and continual development of the Enterprise Architecture and therefore, it includes a detailed architecture development method (TOGAF ADM) and a set of tools. Today, the Zachman Framework has become a de facto standard for classifying the artifacts of Enterprise Architecture, which is also accepted by The Open Group, whose goal with TOGAF is to make the TOGAF ADM a standard method for developing the Enterprise Architecture.

NIEMANN (2005) summarizes the benefits of applying an Enterprise Architecture Framework as their publishers promote them: management of complexity, efficiency gains and increased homogeneity through consolidation as well as shorter development cycles.[18] Both Enterprise Architecture Frameworks have to be used in conjunction to support IT investment decisions from the enterprise view by combining Zachman's way of thinking with an architecture management process for initial and continual development. The Open Group provides a mapping of the TOGAF ADM to the corresponding cells in the Zachman Framework.[19] The usability of an Enterprise

---

[16] cf. The Open Group: TOGAF 8.1 2004
[17] cf. Zachman: The challenge is change 1996, p. 2 f.
[18] cf. Niemann: Unternehmensarchitektur 2005, p. 51
[19] cf. The Open Group: TOGAF Zachman mapping 2002

Architecture depends on the alignment to the enterprises strategic goals and objectives as well as on the measures planned to reach them.[20] In other words, the Enterprise Architecture is useful, if every strategic goal can be found therein. Additionally, the quality of the architecture management process influences the transformation and realization of the strategy.

2.1.2 The Zachman Framework

The Zachman Framework, as shown in figure 1, is a matrix consisting of six rows and six columns, forming 36 cells.

	Data (what?)	Function (how?)	Network (where?)	People (who?)	Time (when?)	Motivation (why?)
Scope (contextual)	Identify entities	Identify business processes	Map of business locations	Identify agents	List significant events	Business goals and strategy
Business Model (conceptual)	Semantic data model	Business process model	Business logistics	Workflow model	Master schedule	Business plan
System Model (logical)	Logical data model	Application architecture	Distributed system architecture	Human interface architecture	Processing structure	Business rule model
Technology Model (physical)	Physical data model	System design	Technology architecture	Human technology interface	Control structure	Business rule design
Detailed Representations (out-of-context)	Database Schema	Program	Network architecture	Security architecture	Timing definition	Business rule specification
Functioning Enterprise	Database	Function	Network	Organization	Schedule	Strategy

Figure 1: The Zachman Framework[21]

To cover the entire organization, the idea of Zachman's framework is to describe the Enterprise Architecture from different viewpoints (representing different roles), regarding several aspects at each stage, resulting in a whole range of documents (e.g. diagrams, charts, models etc.), using uniform vocabulary and a given set of rules.[22] The

---

[20] cf. Masak: Enterprise Architekturen 2005, p. 34
[21] cf. Zachman: Enterprise Architecture Framework 2001
[22] cf. Zachman: Framework for Information Systems Architecture 1987

six rows represent different architectural views on the system during the development process:[23]

- Scope (contextual):
  The senior executive's view, representing the organization's boundaries and connections to the environment.
- Business model (conceptual):
  Description of models and architectures used by owners of business processes.
- System model (logical):
  Description of models and architectures used by engineers, architects and those who determine between what is functionally desirable and what is technically possible.
- Technology model (physical):
  Description of models and architectures used by technicians, engineers and designers who create the actual product.
- Detailed representations (out-of-context perspective):
  Description of the final product or parts included in it (e.g. software components).
- Functioning enterprise (real world):
  Representation of the actual deployed or running elements, data, and people of the organization. It is the underlying of all the abstract perspectives above.

The views have to be processed top-down, while moving the focus from business to technology. Each view has to be examined concerning data (what?), functions (how?), network (where?), people (who?), time (when?) and motivation (why?), meaning different types of abstraction.[24]

The Zachman Framework does not include any tools and it does not dictate to employ specific methods. It can be seen as a checklist to ensure, that all aspects (every view at

---

[23] cf. Frankel et al.: Zachman and MDA 2003, p. 2 f.
[24] cf. Masak: Enterprise Architekturen 2005, p. 35

every stage) of the Enterprise Architecture have been covered.[25] It provides a logical structure for classifying and organizing those elements of an enterprise that are significant to both, managing the enterprise and developing its information systems. By its simple and straightforward approach to address the complexity of today's information systems, the Zachman Framework works as a communications device.[26] The strength of the Zachman Framework is to provide a way of thinking about the Enterprise Architecture in an organized way.

2.1.3 The Open Group Architecture Framework (TOGAF)

As mentioned before, unlike the Zachman Framework, TOGAF contains a detailed method and a set of supporting tools to develop the Enterprise Architecture. The method describes how to design an information system as a set of consistent building blocks. Furthermore, TOGAF offers a list of recommended standards and compliant products that can be used to implement the Enterprise Architecture. In opposite to Zachman, TOGAF does not prescribe a specific set of architectural views, but supports the architect by providing guidelines and examples for developing views.

To architect the entire organization, covering both business and IT, in TOGAF the Enterprise Architecture consists of the following closely interrelated subsets:[27]

- Business architecture:
    Defines the business strategy, governance, organization, and key business processes.
- Application architecture:
    Provides a blueprint for the individual application systems to be deployed, their interactions, and their relationships to the core business processes of the organization.
- Data architecture:
    Describes the structure of an organization's logical and physical data assets and

---

[25] cf. Wiemers et al.: Entscheidungsfall Vorgehensmodell 2005, p. 204 ff.
[26] cf. Zachman: The challenge is change 1996, p. 2 f.
[27] cf. The Open Group: TOGAF 8.1 2004

data management resources.

- Technology architecture:
  Describes the software infrastructure intended to support the deployment of core, mission-critical applications.

TOGAF consists of three main parts, the TOGAF ADM, the TOGAF Enterprise Continuum, and the TOGAF Resource Base, which are described shortly in the following paragraphs.

The Architecture Development Method (ADM)

The ADM is the core component of TOGAF. It defines the process for developing, implementing, and maintaining an organization's Enterprise Architecture, using a step-by-step approach.

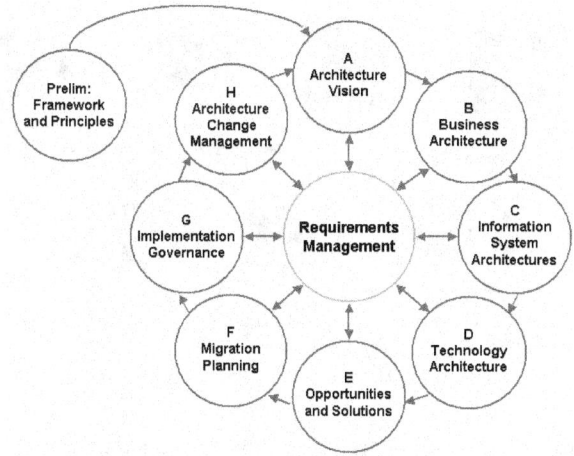

Figure 2: TOGAF ADM basic structure[28]

The phases of the ADM basic structure (figure 2) are passed through iteratively. Each one is further divided into steps, which are processed iterative again. Thereby, frequent

---

[28] cf. The Open Group: TOGAF 8.1 2004

validation of results against the original expectations is ensured. A detailed description of the ADM would be too voluminous for this work, but it has to be remarked, that all phases relate to the business requirements.[29] The ADM is a generic method and has to be customized in order to support an organization-specific Enterprise Architecture. In chapter 4 of this book, a simplified version of Detecon's Enterprise Architecture Management Process will be presented. It is limited to the degree of detail needed to show the linkage to the controlling model.

Enterprise Continuum

By applying the TOGAF ADM, the Enterprise Architecture is developed across the TOGAF Enterprise Continuum, which is shown in figure 3.

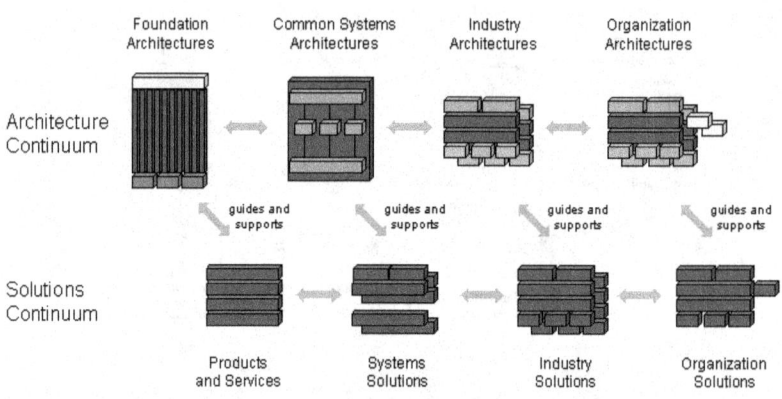

Figure 3: TOGAF Enterprise Continuum[30]

The Enterprise Continuum is a combination of two complementary concepts: the Architecture Continuum and the Solutions Continuum. The Architecture Continuum offers a consistent way to define and to understand the generic rules, representations, and relationships in an information system. It represents a structure of reusable

---

[29] A detailed description of each phase and the corresponding steps can be found on the TOGAF website.
[30] cf. The Open Group: TOGAF 8.1 2004

architecture assets. The Solutions Continuum defines which reusable assets are available in the organizational environment and it provides a consistent way to describe and to understand the implementation of the Architecture Continuum.

The Enterprise Continuum ranges from foundational architectures, over common systems architectures and industry-specific architectures, to an enterprise's own individual Enterprise Architecture. Foundation Architectures are generic architectural models, like the TOGAF Technical Reference Model (TRM). Common Systems Architectures are still generic, but focused on specific technology areas. Industry Architectures are models, which are more closely aligned with industry specific topics. The Organization Architecture is selected according to an individual business model and strategy.

The TOGAF Enterprise Continuum is also connected to the TOGAF Standards Information Base (SIB), which is a database of open industry standards available to define the particular services and other components of an organization-specific architecture.

TOGAF Resource Base

The third component of TOGAF is the TOGAF Resource Base, containing a set of tools and techniques, guidelines, templates, case studies, and background information, helping the architect to apply TOGAF and the TOGAF ADM.[31]

2.2 Service Oriented Architecture

2.2.1 Introduction to SOA

SOA, as it is understood today, became a significant architectural style after the invention of web service technology.[32] In April 2006, the findings of a study, conducted by Forrester, illustrated that especially large and technology-driven enterprises increasingly adopt SOA and 70 % of actual users want to increase SOA usage, which

---

[31] cf. Lankhorst et al.: Enterprise Architecture 2005, p. 25
[32] cf. Erl: Service-Oriented Architecture 2005, p. 74 f.

implies a high degree of satisfaction.[33] A widely known example for SOA is SAP's NetWeaver solution, which is the integration platform to implement SAP's Enterprise Services Architecture (ESA) blueprint.[34]

The roots of SOA can be found in programming paradigms, distribution technology, and business computing.[35] Programming paradigms advanced from functional decomposition, over modularization and object-orientation, to component programming, while continually increasing separation, abstraction, and encapsulation. In combination with the perpetual enhancement of distribution technologies, they contributed to the technical foundation of SOA through proven concepts, as well as by lessons learned. The evolution of business computing, driven by changes in the market environment, lead to the development of complex business applications such as Enterprise Resource Planning (ERP) and Supply Chain Management (SCM), as well as highly specialized solutions for Customer Relationship Management (CRM) and core competency support. These application solutions are strongly dependent on enterprise-wide integration of data and functionality. SOA tries to overcome the inflexibility of former paradigms by improving reusability of business logic and sustainability of data.[36] The central innovation is the appropriateness of the service concept for the business domain, as well as for the IT domain, while enabling Enterprise Application Integration (EAI) to support modern business solutions.

In this chapter, definitions for *'service'* and *'Service Oriented Architecture'* (SOA), based on the key characteristics of the paradigm of *'service orientation'*, are given. Furthermore, the benefits of SOA adoption are shown and the appropriateness of SOA to implement the Enterprise Architecture is explained. Keeping in mind that the goal of this work is to develop a controlling model, it is reasonable to limit the scope of a SOA analysis and description to the business-related attributes. Therefore, SOA

---

[33] cf. Forrester Research: Time for SOA 2006
[34] cf. SAP: NetWeaver 2005, p. 3
[35] cf. Krafzig/Banke/Slama: Enterprise SOA 2005, p. 15 ff.
[36] cf. Krafzig/Banke/Slama: Enterprise SOA 2005, p. 24

2.2.2 Definition of service orientation

The best way to describe SOA is to start with the underlying paradigm of *'service orientation'* to provide the basis for the definition of a *'service'* and *'Service Oriented Architecture'*.

The *'service orientation'* paradigm can be described by its commonly accepted principles:[38]

- *Loose coupling:*
  Services minimize dependencies, only retaining awareness of other services.
- *Autonomy:*
  Services control their encapsulated logic.
- *Abstraction:*
  Services hide internal logic from the outside world.
- *Reusability:*
  Logic is divided with the intention of promoting reuse.
- *Composability:*
  A collection of services can be coordinated and assembled to form composite solutions.
- *Service contract:*
  Services adhere to a contractual agreement designed by service descriptions.
- *Statelessness:*
  Services minimize retaining information specific to an activity.
- *Discoverability:*
  Services can be found and assessed via available discovery mechanisms.

---

[37] A detailed description of SOA technologies and implementation can be found in Erl: Service-Oriented Architecture 2005.
[38] cf. Erl: Service-Oriented Architecture 2005, p. 36 f.

A very general definition for *'service'* is

> "... *a logical unit that accepts requests and returns responses through an interface ...*",[39]

designed on the basis of the principles mentioned above. A business-oriented service is typically concerned with a major aspect of business, e.g. a business entity, a business function, or a business process.[40] The principle of abstraction is often called 'black box', because from the client perspective, it cannot be seen how the service is implemented.[41]

Many different definitions for SOA can be found in literature and some of them are contradictory or inconsistent with others.[42] The definitions span from SOA as a programming paradigm, over SOA as an application architecture, to SOA as an approach to Enterprise Architecture.[43] For this work a definition of SOA from the perspective of Enterprise Architecture is needed. In the previous chapter on Enterprise Architecture, the term *'architecture'* has already been defined referring to TOGAF and the consistency with a widely accepted standard.

Combining the given definition with the paradigm of *'service orientation'*, a *'Service Oriented Architecture'* is

> "... *an architecture, that adheres to the principles of service orientation.*"[44]

When using SOA to implement the Enterprise Architecture, building blocks are used as service modeling units for composition or decomposition of the service-oriented enterprise.[45] They are, very generally speaking, an independent package of functionality, defined to provide one or more services. The term building block fits in great to the composite nature of SOA. Combining the building block approach with the definition derived above, an Enterprise Architecture implemented through SOA can be

---

[39] cf. Oey/Wagner/Rehbach/Bachmann: Serviceorientierte Architekturen 2005, p. 205 f.
[40] cf. Krafzig/Banke/Slama: Enterprise SOA 2005, p. 67
[41] cf. Woods: Enterprise Services Architecture 2004, p. 25
[42] cf. Natis: Service Oriented Architecture 2004, p. 23 ff.
[43] cf. Morgenthal: The A in SOA 2006
[44] Erl: Service-Oriented Architecture 2005, p. 54
[45] cf. Erl: Service-Oriented Architecture 2005, p. 424

characterized as a set of modularized and loosely coupled building blocks, which provide and use services, organized in a multi layered system that is integrated enterprise-wide. For this work, the building block is a very important object of investigation and a detailed description of TOGAF's building block concept is given in chapter 3.2. The SOA layer model, which structures the enterprise's building blocks into functional layers, will be analyzed in chapter 4.3. The holistic approach of Enterprise Architecture demands for enterprise-wide integration of building blocks. This is necessary to realize benefits of SOA across different LOBs and to enable controlling on enterprise level.

Operation of SOA requires Service Management based on a Service Repository and Service Level Agreements (SLA). The Service Repository provides functionality to discover services and it offers all information needed to use the services, such as physical location, information about the service provider, contact person, usage fees, technical constraints, security issues, and available service levels.[46] Therefore, SLAs are a very important connector between IT supply and IT demand. They provide the contractual basis for cooperation.

A *'Service Level Agreement'* can be defined as

> *"A written agreement between an IT service provider and the customer that documents agreed service levels for an IT service."*[47]

SLAs should be business-focused, not technically focused, to comprehensibly communicate the costs and benefits of a service to all parties involved.[48]

2.2.3 Benefits of SOA

The major goal of SOA is to increase *'business agility'*, which can be defined as

> *"The ability to adapt business operations quickly and accurately in response to changes in the business environment."*[49]

---

[46] cf. Krafzig/Banke/Slama: Enterprise SOA 2005, p. 60 f.
[47] cf. Niessen/Oldenburg: Service Level Management 1997, p. 76
[48] cf. Bieberstein et al.: SOA compass 2006, p. 172
[49] Pulier/Taylor: Enterprise SOA 2006, p. 103

An enterprise with a high level of business agility is also called 'adaptive enterprise' or 'agile enterprise'.[50] The fact that enterprises have to adapt to changes, not once in larger temporal intervals, but permanently, has been widely accepted.[51] Some authors state, that SOA will be capable to realize the 'real-time enterprise'.[52] However called, SOA provides a flexible IT infrastructure to realize the vision of a flexible enterprise, which is capable of dealing with the ever changing business environment by continually adapting to changes. Having the flexibility to meet new market demands and to seize opportunities ahead of competitors is one of the most valuable potentials for an enterprise.[53] NIEMANN (2005) states, that business agility is the determining factor to ensure an enterprise's survival in the long run.[54]

Business agility is achieved by the key characteristics of SOA:[55]

- Business IT alignment
- Independence from technology, vendor and product, enabling best-of-breed interoperability
- Reusability
- Flexible sourcing decisions and collaboration possibilities
- Evolutionary approach
- Feedback and contribution at different levels and from different domains

They are described in the following paragraphs. Obviously, the single characteristics cannot be described completely separated, because they are interdependent. An overview is given in figure 4, emphasizing that the beneficial characteristics of SOA foster flexibility of IT and they lead to increased business agility.

---

[50] cf. Butler Group: Enterprise Architecture 2004, p. 10 and p. 29
    The Butler Group as one example uses both terms in one publication.
[51] ct. Aier/Schönherr: EAI als Enabler 2004, p. 69
[52] cf. Schmale: Real-Time Enterprise 2004,
    The term 'Real-time enterprise' was initially coined by the Gartner Group.
[53] cf. Bieberstein et al.: SOA compass 2006, p. 12
[54] cf. Niemann: Unternehmensarchitektur 2005, p. 91 and p. 213
[55] cf. Krafzig/Banke/Slama: Enterprise SOA 2005, p. 239 ff.

Description of the architectural environment   33

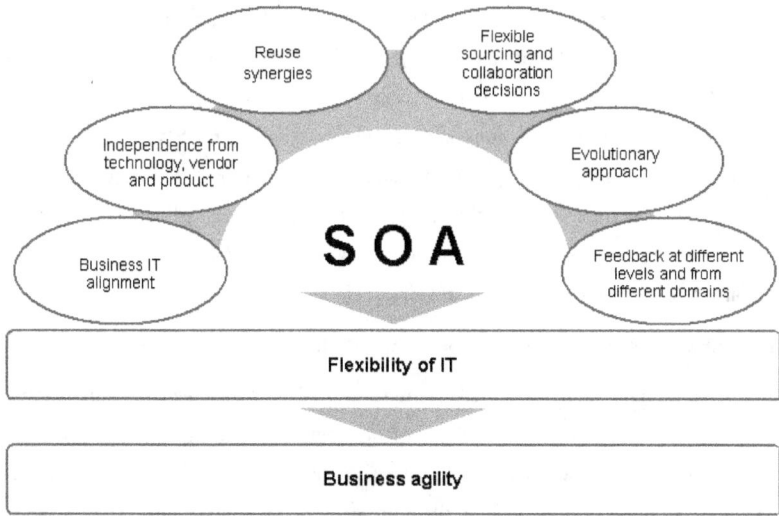

Figure 4: SOA fosters business agility[56]

Business IT alignment

Today, most business activities cannot be performed without IT anymore, because IT evolved from an instrument to an integral part of business.[57] Electronic markets (such as Amazon, Ebay, but also B2B markets) could not even exist without IT, but also telecommunication companies and financial service providers get more and more IT-dependent. Therefore, business strategy and IT strategy have to be aligned and IT strategy has to be planned in conjunction with the enterprise's business objectives.[58] This is called *'business IT alignment'* and it is ensured by coordinating and synchronizing strategic IT controlling with the enterprise's business strategy.[59] The functionality provided by traditional, monolithic applications was inflexible. Whenever the business strategy changed, the emerging business requirements could not be supported adequately anymore. The implementation of marginal changes often led to

---

[56] own figure
[57] cf. Porter/Millar: Competitive Advantage 1985, p. 151ff.
[58] cf. Horváth/Rieg: strategisches IT-Controlling 2001, p. 10 f.
[59] cf. Niemann: Unternehmensarchitektur 2005, p. 57 f.

substantial efforts, resulting in high costs. With SOA, the enterprise's IT gets more flexible and thus, it can be continually aligned with business strategy. Therefore, when using SOA to implement the Enterprise Architecture, the focus lies on the support of business goals and resulting requirements for the technical infrastructure.[60] Planning is usually driven by business requirements and resulting business services, not by the technical infrastructure.[61] Nevertheless, IT can act as an enabler if new technologies provide opportunities for conducting business. Therefore, optimal IT business alignment can only be achieved with concurrent planning.

Independence from technology, vendor and products

SOA enables requirement-oriented combination of 'best-of-breed' products to an individual solution. Earlier mechanisms of distributed computing did not allow for a flexible choice of products due to proprietary communication solutions. SOA promises the ability to solve the interoperability problem by applying platform independent standards of web service communication.[62] Being independent from technology, additionally reduces dependence from vendors. However promised in contemporary technology, there are some incompatibilities (e.g. Sun's J2EE and Microsoft's .NET), which hamper the creation and maintenance of business processes, and it is impossible to eliminate all technology dependencies.[63] Especially the service infrastructure platform, which is central for any SOA implementation, produces a certain degree of dependency. Thus, the vendor dependence is partly relocated from applications to the infrastructure. As a matter of fact, heterogeneity of technology, vendors, and products increases with the size of the enterprise, thus increasing complexity. SOA does not intend to fight heterogeneity, but tries to manage and handle it in a way that it cannot diminish but foster an enterprise's agility.[64]

Reuse synergies and resulting benefits

For a fairly long time, the application of class libraries or code templates at build-time

---

[60] cf. Oey/Wagner/Rehbach/Bachmann: Serviceorientierte Architekturen 2005, p. 210
[61] cf. Krafzig/Banke/Slama: Enterprise SOA 2005, p. 67
[62] cf. Pulier/Taylor: Enterprise SOA 2006, p. 22
[63] cf. Krafzig/Banke/Slama: Enterprise SOA 2005, p. 246
[64] cf. Krafzig/Banke/Slama: Enterprise SOA 2005, p. 242 and 246

facilitates the reuse of code which leads to reduced risk of failure in implementation projects. This is not a new potential of SOA. However, SOA also enables reuse of code and descriptions on this low level by promoting the implementation of reusable software components.[65] But it is important to understand that SOA enables synergies through reuse benefits on the level of a building block.[66] This second type of reuse is the one that is central to the motivation of business agility and the one that is relevant when using SOA to implement the Enterprise Architecture. The decoupling of business rules, business data, and business processes from technology also enables reuse benefits on a non-technological level. Remembering the fact that each building block contains the business data layer, linking it to the different lines of business also ensures data integrity by minimizing data redundancies and inconsistencies. The use of abstract and implementation(-language)-independent interfaces enables reuse even across different technical infrastructures. Data with enterprise-wide relevance has to be made available centrally. Thereby, SOA ensures sustainability of the very important asset information.

The benefits of SOA, that emerge from reuse of existing building blocks, can be summarized to:[67]

- Reduced effort in planning and implementation[68]
- Risk mitigation[69]
- Sustainability of investments[70]
- Higher productivity of solution development[71]

Over time, an enterprise using SOA will establish a sustainable repository of flexible building blocks and services, which can be continually reused. Consequently, reuse benefits will increase during the time of SOA operation. A general assumption of increased quality cannot be made due to problems of reuse when diverting building

---

[65] cf. Erl: Service-Oriented Architecture 2005, p. 100
[66] cf. Krafzig/Banke/Slama: Enterprise SOA 2005, p. 244 f.
[67] Most publications on SOA contain all of the benefits mentioned. Hence, citations refer to the most valuable sources for additional information.
[68] cf. Aier/Dogan: Nachhaltigkeit 2004, p. 101
[69] cf. Krafzig/Banke/Slama: Enterprise SOA 2005, p. 249 f.
[70] cf. Aier/Dogan: Nachhaltigkeit 2004, p. 90 ff.
[71] cf. Krcmar: Informationsmanagement 2005, p. 191

blocks from their initially intended purpose.[72]

Flexible sourcing and collaboration decisions

As another important characteristic, SOA supports efficient sourcing strategies. In 2004, results of market study showed, that 37 % of German enterprises (especially firms with more than 1000 employees) already outsourced substantial parts of their IT.[73] SOA makes sourcing decisions more flexible. In the ideal case, even a single service can be procured and used instantly based on SLAs. The combination of SOA and flexible sourcing definitely increases business agility. However, after the hype on outsourcing in the last years, analysts accepted that it is not a panacea for efficiency problems in IT. Although SOA enables efficient and flexible sourcing, it is important to point out that sourcing decision can also lead to an internal solution or to in-sourcing of an externally provided service.

On the business level, SOA increases interoperation and collaboration possibilities. IT plays a very important role to support intercompany cooperation, through integration of functionality and relevant data across enterprise borders, in order to support collaborative business processes.[74] Often this integration is limited to single applications or functions, whereas SOA enables integration of the infrastructure. B2B commerce can be implemented flexibly and economically.[75] SOA supports the creation of new products and services, enterprise-internal by enabling the reuse of existing services, as well as across enterprise boundaries by allowing for ad hoc liaisons.[76] Additionally, SOA facilitates communication with other enterprises according to the available services.[77] The improved possibility of interoperation and collaboration with business partners fosters innovation by enabling better exploitation of emerging business opportunities.

---

[72] cf. Aier/Dogan: Nachhaltigkeit 2004, p. 101
[73] cf. TechConsult/Lünendonk: Outsourcing Services 2004
[74] cf. Berger/Lehner: Prozesskopplung 2002, p. 281
[75] cf. Pulier/Taylor: Enterprise SOA 2006, p. 73 ff.
[76] cf. Lankhorst et al.: Enterprise Architecture 2005, p. 44 f.
[77] cf. Arsanjani: Service-oriented modeling 2005

Evolutionary Approach

As already mentioned, traditional IT applications were inflexible and they had to be reengineered in large-scale projects to support a changing business strategy or new business processes. Enterprises do not intend to implement an architecture as a "big bang" project.[78] Consequently, the introduction of SOA is not a one-off project[79] and the benefits mentioned above will not become apparent instantly. SOA enables an evolutionary step-by-step approach of Enterprise Architecture Management, allowing for stepwise migration and continual advancements. Adopting SOA will bring some quick-wins in the beginning and benefits will steadily evolve during the implementation process.

Today, most SOA implementations are limited to a certain part of the Enterprise Architecture. This does not mean that SOA adoption does not comprise the whole enterprise, but that legacy systems still exist, encapsulated through services to ensure integration. The evolutionary approach of SOA allows for several options for an enterprise to start with SOA adoption:[80]

- Initial adoption:
  Assessment of SOA readiness regarding the capability to transform or integrate legacy systems.
- LOB adoption:
  Identification a LOB and prioritize activities where business agility increases business value.
- Enterprise adoption:
  Enterprise-wide prioritization of activities.
- Enterprise and partner network adoption:
  Additional involvement of the enterprise's business partners, suppliers or customers.

To ensure a smooth migration to SOA, every enterprise has to develop an organizational

---

[78] cf. Bieberstein et al.: SOA compass 2006, p. 6
[79] cf. Krafzig/Banke/Slama: Enterprise SOA 2005, p. 263
[80] cf. Bieberstein et al.: SOA compass 2006, p. 66

SOA roadmap.[81] When operating SOA, the definition and application of an architecture development process results in additional simplification of the development process.[82] The TOGAF ADM, as presented in chapter 2.1.3, is one reference to design an enterprise-specific architecture development process. Benefits of an evolutionary approach are closely related to reuse synergies and they result in reduced implementation risk of failure and a higher capacity for change by reusing proven building blocks.

Feedback and Contribution at different levels and from different domains

The holistic approach of Enterprise Architecture impacts all levels of the organization. To ensure that the Enterprise Architecture fulfills the requirements and key needs of all stakeholders, they should be able to contribute to the architecture. The idea is to achieve optimal IT support through concurrent planning of IT solutions. Therefore, Enterprise Architecture has to be made understandable to every stakeholder in order to access knowledge of the entire enterprise.

In addition, the application of an Enterprise Architecture Framework ensures completeness of analysis. SOA supports communication by providing abstractions on different levels in order to enable both, functional departments and IT experts, to contribute to valuable Enterprise Architecture development.[83]

2.2.4 Potential cost savings through SOA

Cost efficiency plays a key role in price-sensitive, low margin, and mature markets with limited product innovation possibilities. Offering the lowest price can be a competitive advantage. A differentiation between direct savings of IT costs and indirect savings of business costs can be made.[84] Savings at business level are closely related to business agility, for example, savings through freedom of choice of service providers. Faster resource-efficient choosing supports business process change. In addition, competition between external service providers will result in lower prices, leading to a reduction of

---

[81] cf. Pulier/Taylor: Enterprise SOA 2006, p. 229
[82] cf. Krafzig/Banke/Slama: Enterprise SOA 2005, p. 239
[83] cf. Krafzig/Banke/Slama: Enterprise SOA 2005, p. 249
[84] cf. Krafzig/Banke/Slama: Enterprise SOA 2005, p. 243

costs.[85]

Most sources for IT cost savings are closely related to the higher degree of reusability, for example, reduced project costs due to more efficient implementation and deployment, simplification of business process modification, or optimization and sustainability of investments. However, it has to be pointed out, that the adoption of SOA requires major capital investments at the beginning, which has to be taken into account when calculating for the return on investment (ROI) of SOA.[86]

2.3 Enterprise Architecture and SOA

As we have seen in the previous subchapter, SOA is one possibility to implement a flexible Enterprise Architecture. On the one hand, since Enterprise Architecture covers both, business and IT, it has to be shown, that the service concept is as appropriate for the business domain as it is for the IT domain. On the other hand, the adoption of SOA requires Enterprise Architecture Management and Enterprise Architecture has to guide SOA adoption.[87] Enterprise Architecture Management methods have to be verified regarding their applicability to manage SOA services. In case they are not, they have to be adapted or new methods have to be used.

It has to be emphasized, that SOA is not a technology as much as it is a way of thinking.[88] The design philosophy can be used and understood in both domains and it can be equally applied to a task, a solution, an enterprise, or a community.[89] If an appropriate granularity is chosen, services do not confuse business practitioners by presenting too much detail.[90] Therefore, it can build the foundation for a mutual language and it can facilitate communication,[91] which is also a goal of Enterprise Architecture. SOA is getting successful because it focuses on business processes and

---

[85] cf. Lankhorst et al.: Enterprise Architecture 2005, p. 44
[86] cf. Schmelzer: ROI of SOA 2006, p. 2 ff.
[87] cf. Forrester Research: Enterprise Architecture of SOA 2006, p. 1
[88] cf. Groves: Planning SOA 2005
[89] cf. Schekkerman: Service Oriented Architecture 2006
[90] cf. Krafzig/Banke/Slama: Enterprise SOA 2005, p. 242
[91] cf. Lankhorst et al.: Enterprise Architecture 2005, p. 44

how technology can be used to support them.[92] In former years, a frequent mistake was to assign roles the other way around. But IT can also be the enabler for new business opportunities.

If applied in conjunction with Enterprise Architecture, SOA can be the key to achieve ultimate flexibility in business and IT design, and it provides a closer alignment between business and IT systems. To profit from business agility and business IT alignment, communication between both domains has to be facilitated in order to ensure a complete reflection of business requirements in IT supply.[93]

The definitions given in the previous chapter show that the intention of Enterprise Architecture is management of an enterprise's IT assets and their relationships. The TOGAF definition uses the word 'component', which can be understood as a synonym for asset.[94] When adopting SOA, the enterprise's IT is split-up into services. Thus, they are the enterprise's components or respectively its IT assets that have to be managed. The goal of adopting SOA is to apply the service concept conceptually and practically throughout the enterprise's IT.[95] SOA itself does not replace the Enterprise Architecture, but it influences its organization and design. Due to their finer granularity, the number of services with SOA will be higher than the number of components in a classical IT environment, leading to increased complexity. Therefore, Enterprise Architecture is not only applicable for managing SOA, in fact it is indispensable for efficient operation. While SOA introduces a new design philosophy, it does not require a new approach to Enterprise Architecture, but its special characteristics have to be considered in Enterprise Architecture Management.[96] This includes the adoption of SOA-appropriate controlling methods.

A project-driven approach on enterprise level, like Detecon's TOGAF-based Architecture Management Process (figure 5), links business strategy to the enterprise's LOBs, which enables an efficient operation of SOA.

---

[92] cf. Burkhard/Laures: SOA Paradigma 2003, p. 16
[93] cf. Bieberstein et al.: SOA compass 2006: , p. 68
[94] cf. chapter 2.1.1
[95] cf. Gallas/Schönherr: Service Management 2005, p. 228
[96] cf. Forrester Research: Enterprise Architecture of SOA 2006, p. 2

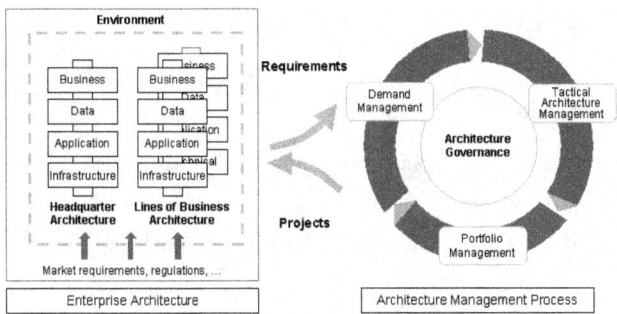

Figure 5: Enterprise Architecture Management for SOA[97]

---

[97] cf. Weber/Schmidtmann: Concurrent Planning 2006, p. 29

3 IT controlling

3.1 Introduction to controlling

To reach the goal of developing a controlling model, the underlying definition of controlling and IT controlling has to be given, and the tasks assigned have to be described. According to the International Group of Controlling (IGC), *'controlling'* provides

> *"... an accompanying service in management accounting and financial analyses for managers which enables them to plan and control their operations according to objectives."*[98]

This implies the following tasks:[99]

- Responsibility for the transparency of business results, finance, processes, and strategy, thus contributing to higher profitability.
- Coordination of sub-targets and sub-plans in a holistic way and organizing a reporting-system which is future-oriented and covers the business as whole.
- Moderation of the controlling process so that every decision maker can act in accordance with agreed objectives.
- Ensure that managers receive all necessary information.
- Create and maintain the controlling system.

Summarized, controlling is seen as an internal economic advisor to provide transparency and to ensure consistent definition, communication, and verification of an enterprise's goals and objectives. These main characteristics of controlling can also be found in other publications. Based on several academic and practical studies on controlling, HORVÁTH (2004) summarizes, that it is a subsystem of corporate management.[100] For KARGL (1996) controlling has the responsibility to provide transparency as a support function for corporate management, which is responsible for

---

[98] International Group of Controlling: Mission Statement 2001
[99] cf. Koslowski/Kohlmeier: Controlling Wörterbuch 2001, p. V
[100] cf. Horváth: Controlling 2004, p. 151 f.

decision making.[101] Both are shorter definitions, but consistent with IGC's perception of controlling. Referring to HORVÁTH (2004), controlling tasks are performed to ensure the ability to coordinate, to react, and to adapt in order to reach the enterprise's objectives.[102] Thus, controlling ensures the enterprise's survival and future development.

3.2 IT controlling

3.2.1 Structure of IT controlling

This section addresses IT controlling issues in the architectural environment as described in the previous chapters. Basically, the given description of controlling can also be transferred to IT controlling. IT controlling is not a closed system, because it covers more than one management system with different goals and objectives.[103] In general, IT service provider and IT service user are located in different organizational units. IT controlling does not only cover the IT domain itself, but also affects all parts of the enterprise that use IT systems.

IT Performance Management is not limited to IT supply, but has to be conducted in conjunction with IT demand in order to achieve economic efficiency and effectiveness of IT. This can also be seen in the following definition:

> "IT Performance Management addresses the way organizations should balance the demand and the supply of information technology, optimizing the cost and maximizing the business value of IT."[104]

KÜTZ (2005) describes a very useful categorization of IT controlling, taking this organizational separation into account. Accordingly, IT controlling can be divided into three parts, covering IT supply and IT demand while ensuring regulation and supervision through IT governance.[105] Figure 6 shows the relationships between these

---

[101] cf. Kargl: Controlling 1996, p. 5 ff.
[102] cf. Horváth: Controlling 2004, p. 149
[103] cf. Kütz: IT-Controlling 2005, p. 9 f.
[104] cf. Wiggers et al.: IT Performance Management 2004, p. 24 ff.
[105] cf. Kütz: IT-Controlling 2005, p. 7 f.

three parts and it extends the more general original figure with the missing flow of IT cost information via service prices from IT supply to the IT demand side.

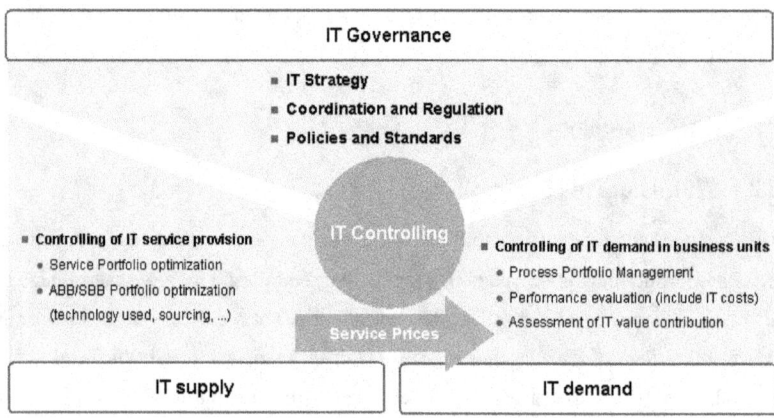

Figure 6: Structure of IT controlling[106]

The three parts of IT controlling and the corresponding tasks in the given architectural environment are described more detailed in the following.

3.2.2 IT supply side: controlling IT service provision

The first part of IT controlling covers the IT supply side, which produces and provides IT services. Normally, there are multiple organization units that perform IT services.[107] IT service providing can be performed enterprise-internal, as well as outside by one or more external IT service providers. Outsourcing is seen as a special case for IT controlling activities on the IT supply side, thus a subchapter is granted to sourcing decisions.[108]

According to traditional organizations, IT projects are performed to develop and

---

[106] own figure, following Kütz: IT-Controlling 2005, p. 8, extended
[107] cf. Kütz: IT-Controlling 2005, p. 15
[108] cf. chapter 5.3

implement IT systems and IT processes are executed to create an IT service.[109] The output generated on the IT supply side is also called IT product.[110] More generally, the term IT asset can be used for any valuable item in the Enterprise Architecture. In the given architectural environment, IT assets generated by the IT supply side can be building blocks and services.[111] Therefore, they are the focus of IT controlling activities. Collecting IT cost information needed for controlling methods such as total cost of ownership (TCO) analysis, IT investment valuation, and benchmarking, allows for active strategic management of IT services and it enables optimization of the enterprise's building block portfolio and service portfolio.

3.2.3   IT demand side: controlling IT service usage

There are multiple organization units in the enterprise that demand IT services. SOA is based on the idea of IT-internal reuse. Thus, to avoid confusion, it has to be distinguished between IT-internal demands and IT-external demands emerging from business units. A clear borderline is ensured by differentiating between reuse of building blocks and services offered to business units. Thus from now on, IT demand side means business units, which use IT services to support their business processes. However, this does not mean that there is no IT-internal charging. In fact, only consistent IT-internal service charging ensures full cost coverage,[112] but this is conducted on the IT supply side.

The IT cost information collected on the IT supply side is transferred to the IT demand side via service prices and it is used as input for controlling methods. Business units become capable of optimizing their business process portfolio, including IT costs and simultaneously assessing IT value contribution. If business unit managers can control IT usage, this can result in more thoughtful use of IT resources.[113] On enterprise level, consideration of IT costs enables consistent performance evaluation of business units. Summarized, IT controlling has to provide consistent IT cost information, presented in

---

[109] cf. Kütz: IT-Controlling 2005, p. 16 ff.
[110] cf. Fernholz/Kielwein/Buresch: IV-Produkt-Controlling 2000, p. 59
[111] cf. Hafner/Schelp/Winter: Architekturmanagement 2004, p. 59
[112] cf. Bradley: IT Costing 2003, p. 3
[113] cf. Gadatsch: IT-Controlling 2005, p. 113 f.

formats, which satisfy multiple recipients.

3.2.4 IT governance

The Organization for Economic Cooperation and Development (OECD) defines, that *'corporate governance'*

> "... *provides the structure through which the objectives of the company are set, and the means of attaining those objectives and monitoring performance are determined.*"[114]

Corporate governance covers six key assets, which enterprises use to accomplish their strategy and to generate business value.[115] These are human assets, financial assets, IT assets, relationship assets, and intellectual property assets. Consequently, *'IT governance'* is the part of corporate governance that controls IT assets.[116] The IT Governance Institute[117] (ITGI) defines:

> "*IT governance is an integral part of corporate governance and consists of the leadership and organizational structures and processes that ensure that the organization's IT sustains and extends the organization's strategies and objectives.*"[118]

Forrester Research introduces a more finance-driven definition:

> "*The process by which decisions are made around IT investments. How decisions are made, who makes the decisions, who is held accountable, and how the results of decisions are measured and monitored are all parts of IT governance.*"[119]

On the basis of the definitions published by the ITGI, NIEMANN (2005) states, that IT governance has to ensure, that IT demands are satisfied, IT resources are continually

---

[114] cf. Organization for Economic Cooperation and Development: Corporate Governance 2004, p. 11
[115] cf. Weill/Ross: IT Governance 2004, p. 6 f.
[116] cf. Lankhorst et al.: Enterprise Architecture 2005, p. 244
[117] The IT Governance Institute (www.itgi.org) was established in 1998 to advance international thinking and standards in directing and controlling an enterprise's information technology.
[118] cf. IT Governance Institute: Board Briefing 2003, p. 10
[119] cf. Forrester Research: IT Governance 2005, p. 3

planned, controlled, and optimized, and IT performance is measured and risks are minimized. This can be summarized to the fact that IT governance considers effectiveness, efficiency, and security.[120] This fact confirms the strong connection between IT controlling, which focuses on the application of methods, and IT governance, which provides the organizational framework. Additionally, IT governance, as one part of corporate governance, ensures the linkage to the enterprise's goals and objectives.

Getting back to the structure of IT controlling, IT governance coordinates IT demand and IT supply, and it provides a framework of regulations and conditions, policies, and standards. Every IT service provider has to adhere to the regulations and conditions given by the enterprise's IT governance.[121]

3.3 Operative versus strategic controlling

Referring to the time horizon of an enterprise's goals, it can be distinguished between *'operative controlling'* and *'strategic controlling'* activities.[122] Operative controlling concentrates on short and medium term issues, whereas strategic controlling focuses on problems that have a long-term impact on the enterprise. Consequently, only strategic controlling offers the ability to react to changes in the environment or to identify problems early enough to put in countermeasures. Strategic controlling has to identify problems before they can be seen in the data collected by operative controlling. This does not mean that strategies and plans last in the long term. Controlling systems must ensure strategic flexibility and strategies have to be constantly reviewed and adjusted if necessary.[123]

Therefore, *'strategic controlling'*

"... *supports the leadership process, by providing relevant information and coordinating strategic planning, strategy realization and strategic control.*"[124]

---

[120] cf. Niemann: Unternehmensarchitektur 2005, p. 29
[121] cf. Kütz: IT-Controlling 2005, p. 15
[122] cf. Horváth: Controlling 2004, p. 150
[123] cf. Horváth: Strategiekompetenz 2000, p. 83 ff.
[124] cf. Horváth/Rieg: strategisches IT-Controlling 2001, p. 9

This distinction made for controlling, based on time horizon and the enterprise's goals and objectives, can be equally transferred to IT controlling.

3.4 Strategic IT controlling

HORVÁTH/RIEG (2001) define three main tasks of strategic IT controlling. First, it has to provide information about the basic strategic options for IT, which mainly depend on the importance of IT for the business conducted. Based on the business strategy and on technological possibilities, a strategic option has to be chosen. Subsequently, as second task, the IT strategy has to be segmented regarding different strategic aspects and the following partial IT strategies have to be derived: IT technology strategy (applied hardware and software technologies, ...), IT infrastructure strategy (networks, operating systems, middleware, ...), IT application strategy (vendors, ...), and IT organization strategy. The third task is strategic IT investment valuation in order to ensure economic efficiency, which is also part of strategic controlling, because a disproportionate restrictive operative economic efficiency control can impede the creation of strategic competitive advantages.[125]

From the financial point of view, every potential investment has to be realized if it increases an enterprise's value.[126] IT investments, in distinction to financial investments, often have non-monetary and intangible benefits, which makes them hard to measure or quantify. In reality, IT investments are subject to irrational decisions as often as other decisions in enterprises are.[127] However, both issues remain unconsidered in this work and evaluation is limited to financial information.

3.5 Special requirements for the given architectural environment

An Enterprise Architecture implementation through SOA can be characterized as a set of modularized and loosely coupled building blocks that provide and use services, which are organized in a multi layered system that is integrated enterprise-wide. Independent from any architectural paradigm, it is necessary to monitor and to control

---

[125] cf. Horváth/Rieg: strategisches IT-Controlling 2001, p. 12 f.
[126] cf. Hardt/Rindler: Wertorientierte Unternehmensführung 2003, p. 276
[127] cf. Mintzberg/Westley: Decision Making 2001, p. 89 f.

the financial aspects of IT. However, the applied controlling methods must be adequate. Therefore, when adopting SOA, a controlling model has to be in place to satisfy the requirements that come from the special characteristics. Since there is no matured controlling model for this kind of architecture, it is the goal of this work to develop a controlling model for the service-oriented Enterprise Architecture.

4 Controlling model development

4.1 How to derive the controlling model

4.1.1 Definition of purposes

Although the chapter on IT controlling introduces more tasks, it is useful to focus on issues related to characteristics of the given architectural environment. From the description of Enterprise Architecture and SOA, we know that the two most striking features are better business IT alignment and increased business agility. Therefore, the controlling model is developed to satisfy two main objectives:

- Increase cost transparency through consistent data and adjusted granularity.
- Increase cost awareness throughout the enterprise, providing measures and units understandable for IT and business units.

Realizing both enables cost calculations, performance assessment, and sourcing decisions, leading to increased IT effectiveness and increased economic efficiency as motivated when introducing IT controlling. On the IT supply side, higher quality and finer granularity of cost information enables more detailed decision making and solution selection. On the IT demand side they affect service selection, resource consumption and allow for better performance valuation.

4.1.2 Basic principles

There are two basic principles that should always be remembered, when developing the controlling model. As previously mentioned, more detailed financial information increases cost transparency and cost awareness, and it yields various direct and indirect benefits. Though excessive cost control can also have drawbacks. Whenever refining the granularity of analyses, it has to be ensured, that the value of information gained exceeds the costs of determination. Therefore, the ratio of costs per information gained and the underlying purpose of analysis should be taken into consideration.[128] The goal is not to determine costs to the last penny, but to give IT a means to reduce costs and

---

[128] cf. Kütz: Kennzahlen der IT 2003, p. 34 ff.

business units a means to control IT costs. Additionally, the method of transferring costs to business units has to be made transparent and comprehensible to everyone involved.

4.1.3 Cost accounting basics

Cost awareness can only be achieved by application of full costing, covering direct and overhead costs. Therefore, this accounting approach is applied in this work. The accounting approach needed for sourcing decisions depends on the actual timeframe of the particular decision. No general statement can be made here. This issue will be discussed in the chapter on sourcing decisions.

'Full costing' can be defined as

> *"Allocation of total costs to units of cost. Direct costs are allocated directly, while overhead expenses are allocated via cost center accounting."*[129]

However, the application of full costing has some drawbacks. The definition of distribution keys for fixed costs or overhead costs can result in inconsistent decision making.[130] In general, cost accounting can be structured into three basic steps:

- Cost element accounting:
  Determination, valuation, and systematic structuring of the enterprise's costs.[131]

- Cost center accounting:
  Analysis where costs come from and preprocessing of overhead expenses for charging to units of costs.[132]

- Unit cost accounting:
  Analysis which of the enterprise's activities accrues costs.[133]

Summarizing, cost accounting activities comprise cost collection, cost distribution, and

---

[129] cf. Schweitzer/Küpper: Kosten- und Erlösrechnung 2003, p. 62
[130] cf. Schweitzer/Küpper: Kosten- und Erlösrechnung 2003, p. 63
Calculation examples, leading to inconsistent decisions can be found in basic accounting literature. A good argumentation can be found in Steger: Kosten- und Leistungsrechnung 2001, p. 343 ff.
[131] cf. Coenenberg: Kostenrechnung 2003, p. 49
[132] cf. Schweitzer/Küpper: Kosten- und Erlösrechnung 2003, p. 127 f. and
cf. Coenenberg: Kostenrechnung 2003, p. 74 f.
[133] cf. Heinen/Dietel Kostenrechnung 1991, p. 1195

calculation of costs and results.[134] This basic structure is helpful as a checklist to ensure, that the developed controlling model includes all three necessary steps.

4.1.4 Definition of objectives

After the purposes of controlling activities, the underlying basic principles and three essential cost accounting steps have been introduced, the objectives of the controlling model have to be defined accordingly.

First, the controlling model must enable the evaluation of building blocks over their entire lifecycle. Unfortunately in practice, IT assets are rarely valuated covering their whole life cycle. Most enterprises focus on the determination of initial development costs, whereas ongoing operating expenses remain unknown.[135] The application of a life cycle model ensures to cover all building block costs, taking operational costs into account.

Second, a SOA-appropriate cost allocation method has to be developed. The allocation of IT costs to business units is also called chargeback.[136] The insufficient ability to calculate costs and benefits of IT investments impedes consistent cost efficiency analyses.[137] A consistent calculation is impossible without a cost allocation method that ensures chargeback to users of services. In fact, the implementation of cost allocation mechanisms is indispensable for justification of IT investments or sourcing decisions.[138] It has to consider IT-internal reuse as well as reuse by the enterprise's business units.

Almost every controlling activity depends on the availability of adequate cost data. This is the third important issue that has to be considered. The required financial information has to be made available in financial controlling systems. The most important question is the granularity of financial analyses. As a heritage from monolithic mainframe systems, even today some enterprises accept IT costs as a large black box. When adopting SOA, the enterprise's IT is split up into smaller components. Thus,

---

[134] cf. Fischer: Kostencontrolling 2000, p. 170
[135] cf. Zarnekow/Brenner: Kosten im Lebenszyklus 2004, p. 338
[136] cf. Weill/Ross: IT Governance 2004, p. 102
[137] cf. Hirnle/Hess: IT-Investitionsentscheidungen 2004, p. 90
[138] cf. Kargl: Controlling 1996, p. 118 ff.

IT controlling has to provide more detailed data, too.

4.2 The building block approach

4.2.1 TOGAF's building block definition

The Enterprise Architecture is broken down into building blocks. This subsection describes the characteristics of building blocks and it is based on the information given on the TOGAF website. After describing the generic characteristics of a building block, a distinction between Architecture Building Blocks (ABB) and Solution Building Blocks (SBB) is made and their relationship is shown.

According to TOGAF, a *'building block'* is

> "... *a package of functionality defined to meet the business needs across an organization."* [139]

It has published interfaces to access the functionality and it may interoperate with other, independent building blocks. Ideally, a building block is reusable, replaceable, and well specified. The Enterprise Architecture describes how functionality, products, and custom developments are assembled into building blocks.

An *'Architecture Building Block'*

> "... *captures business and technical requirements and defines what functionality will be implemented."* [140]

In distinction, a *'Solution Building Block'*

> "... *defines what products and components will implement the functionality to fulfill business requirements."*[141]

An ABB is technology aware, whereas a SBB is product or vendor aware. In TOGAF, an ABB relates to the Architecture Continuum and it is defined or selected as a result of Architecture Development Method (ADM) application. SBBs relate to the Solutions

---

[139] The Open Group: Introduction to Building Blocks 1999
[140] The Open Group: Introduction to Building Blocks 1999
[141] The Open Group: Introduction to Building Blocks 1999

Continuum and they may be either procured or developed.[142] The quality of building block design affects the ability of legacy system integration, interoperability, and flexibility in the creation of new systems and applications.[143]

4.2.2 Decoupling of logical and physical architecture

Decoupling the logical architecture from the physical architecture ensures independency from vendor software solutions and their standards.[144] ABB specification can be reused, when changing the technology used for implementation of the SBB. Another benefit of this abstraction is the decoupling of business life cycles from technology life cycles, which also simplifies the introduction of new technology.[145]

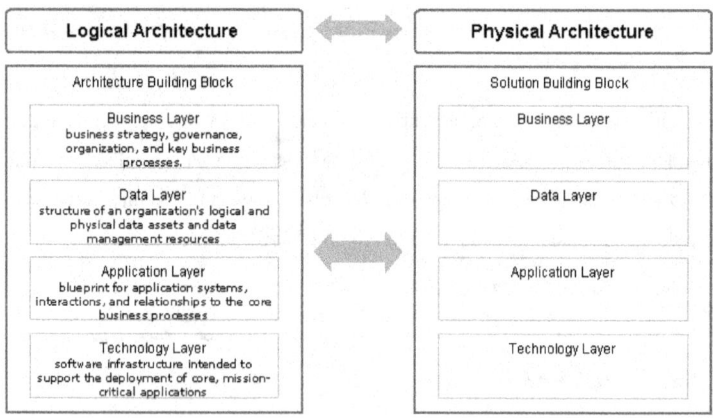

Figure 7: Logical decoupling and building block-internal layers[146]

ABBs are the planning and controlling elements of an IT system, whereas SBBs represent the real physical solution of an ABB. This two-step approach, with logical planning and physical solution selection, avoids redundancy and it leverages synergies

---

[142] cf. chapter 2.1.3: Description of TOGAF and Figure 3: TOGAF Enterprise Continuum
[143] cf. The Open Group: Introduction to Building Blocks 1999
[144] cf. chapter 2.2
[145] cf. Krafzig/Banke/Slama: Enterprise SOA 2005, p. 245 f.
[146] own figure, following The Open Group: TOGAF 8.1 2004

enterprise-wide. In the introductory chapter, the 'business architecture', 'application architecture', 'data architecture', and 'technology architecture' have been defined as subsets of the Enterprise Architecture.[147] As a building block is a package of functionality, defined to meet a business need, it is designed and implemented including all four architectural layers. This applies to ABBs as well as to SBBs. Thereby loose coupling (minimize dependencies to other building blocks) and autonomy (controls the encapsulated logic) is ensured and a certain level of abstraction (hide internal logic from the outside world) is provided.

4.2.3 Enterprise Architecture Management with building blocks

For managing the Enterprise Architecture, a scalable system of planning objects is needed. Therefore, the enterprise's IT is structured in a systematic hierarchical order (figure 8). Accordingly, the IT domain contains one or more IT systems and each IT system consists of one or more building blocks.

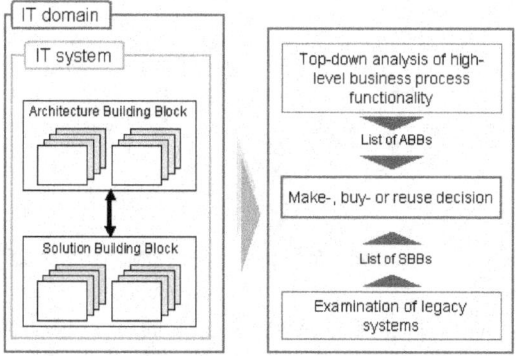

Figure 8: A scalable system of planning objects[148]

This systematic hierarchical order is equally useful for migrating an existing architecture to SOA. A top-down analysis of high-level business process functionality

---

[147] cf. chapter 2.1.3
[148] cf. Detecon: Service Oriented Enterprise Architecture 2006

yields a list of ABBs and services needed. The examination of legacy systems provides a list of existing SBBs and services. On the basis of these two lists, missing elements can be determined and a requirement-oriented make, buy, or reuse decisions can be made. Three categories of building blocks can be defined. There are re-usable building blocks (legacy systems), building blocks to be developed (such as new applications), and building blocks to be purchased (i.e. commercial off-the-shelf applications).[149] Consequently, an ABB directs and guides the development or procurement of the corresponding SBB.

When migrating to SOA, every existing application or system is seen as a legacy application or respectively a legacy system. This view differs from only categorizing monolithic mainframe systems as legacy systems. Obviously, they are included.

4.2.4 Building block ownership

Three necessary concepts for managing SOA and the lifecycle of services must be applied together with the building block approach (figure 9).

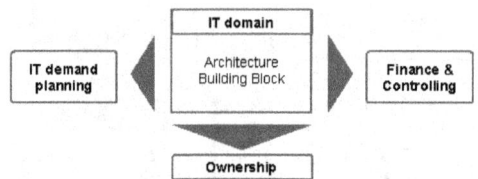

Figure 9: Concepts for Building Block Management[150]

IT demand planning comprises collection of demands and planning of IT support. Building block ownership is part of IT governance and it defines the accountability for maximizing the value of an IT solution.[151] Ownership is independent from organization. In traditional architectures, ownership for applications and data was located in the business unit or operational department, whereas ownership is distributed throughout

---

[149] cf. The Open Group: Building Blocks and the ADM 1998
[150] cf. Detecon: Service Oriented Enterprise Architecture 2006
[151] The concept of building block ownership considers both definitions given for IT governance.

the enterprise when adopting SOA.[152] There can be one or several owners for one building block. The linkage to the enterprise's finance and controlling systems requires the definition of controlling nodes, according to the building block structure. Building blocks and controlling nodes have to be synchronized during their whole lifecycle in order to control the business case.

4.2.5 Granularity of financial analyses

Granularity of financial analyses has to be chosen according to the intended purposes of controlling activities. Therefore, it has to be chosen in order to increase cost transparency and cost awareness. Financial controlling systems must support all relevant decisions. These include financial valuation of ABBs and business services, valuation of legacy systems, as well as sourcing decisions. In addition, granularity provided has to be applicable for valuation of IT usage in business units.

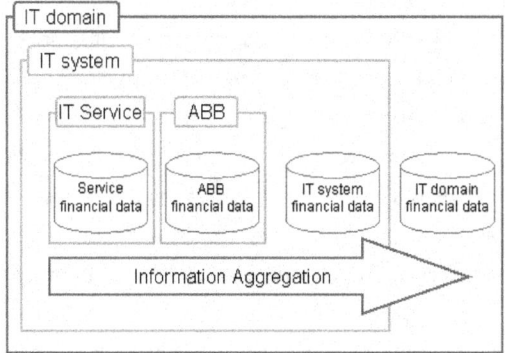

Figure 10: Granularity of financial analyses[153]

The presence of a hierarchical system of planning objects (figure 8) enables aggregation of financial information for single planning objects to any higher level of planning objects. For example, the sum of costs of an IT system's building blocks equals the IT

---

[152] cf. Masak: Enterprise Architekturen 2005, p. 221
[153] own figure

system's costs. Choosing the smallest measurement unit supports both, valuation of single planning objects and aggregation of cost information to a higher level (figure 10). A consistent internal cost allocation method is a prerequisite for correct results when aggregating financial information. Due to the possible relationships between building blocks and services, no general ranking regarding granularity can be made. In fact, a building block can provide multiple services or a service can involve multiple building blocks.[154] Nevertheless, both are included in the above figure. Having financial data about building blocks available allows for calculation of service costs. Thus, ABBs, as the planning and controlling elements in Enterprise Architecture, are the object of further investigation.

4.3 The SOA layer model

4.3.1 Detecon's SOA layer model

The enterprise's building blocks are organized in the SOA layer model. It is important to understand the purpose of architectural layers and why they are beneficial. On the one hand, layers provide a conceptual structure on enterprise level.[155] On the other hand, layers encapsulate the information objects contained.[156] Therefore, they provide a certain level of abstraction between the functionality offered and how this functionality is implemented. In fact, layers are not optional but a prerequisite to realize the benefits of SOA as motivated in chapter 2.2.3.[157] Layers in SOA have to be seen in distinction to physical tiers.[158] For example, not all services of one SOA layer must be deployed at the same location and one location can contain services originated from different layers. The presence of multiple tiers is only one of many characteristics that make the difference between SOA and traditional architectural styles.[159]

Detecon developed a SOA layer model, which will be the foundation for further

---

[154] cf. chapter 4.3 and appendix A
[155] cf. Krafzig/Banke/Slama: Enterprise SOA 2005, p. 82
[156] cf. Lankes/Matthes/Wittenburg: Architekturmanagement 2005, p. 314 f.
[157] cf. Erl: Service-Oriented Architecture 2005, p. 334
[158] cf. Krafzig/Banke/Slama: Enterprise SOA 2005, p. 83
[159] cf. Erl: Service-Oriented Architecture 2005, p. 88 ff.

analyses regarding controlling issues. It structures the Enterprise Architecture into five horizontal layers (figure 11).

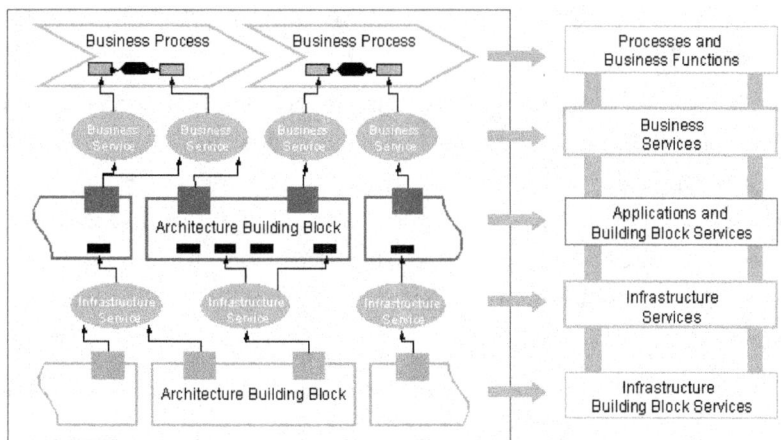

Figure 11: Detecon's SOA layer model[160]

LANKES/MATTHES/WITTENBURG (2005) developed an information model for Enterprise Architecture Management (figure 12).

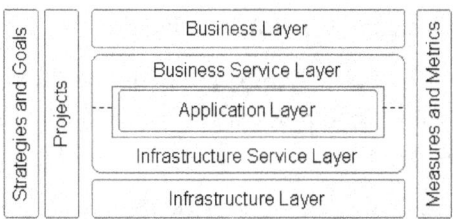

Figure 12: Information model for Enterprise Architecture Management[161]

There are many analogies to Detecon's SOA layer model, which proofs general

---

[160] cf. Detecon: Service Oriented Enterprise Architecture 2006
[161] cf. Lankes/Matthes/Wittenburg: Architekturmanagement 2005, p. 314

applicability. It contains additional cross functions and equivalent horizontal layers, but it does not specify the layer-internal structures.[162] The characteristics of *'business layer'*, *'business service layer'*, *'application layer'*, *'infrastructure service layer'*, and *'infrastructure layer'* can be described as they appear in the model from a bottom-up perspective:[163]

The infrastructure layer consists of infrastructure components. The infrastructure service layer connects the infrastructure layer with the application layer using infrastructure services. The application layer contains the enterprise's business applications. The business service layer connects the application layer with the business layer using business services. Business services as well as infrastructure services are based on SLAs. The business layer contains products, business processes, and organizational units.

Detecon's SOA layer model is based on the building block approach, whereas LANKES/MATTHES/WITTENBURG (2005) do not specify how each layer is organized. Hence, the infrastructure layer, as well as the application layer, consists of a set of building blocks, which provide services realizing the functionality needed in the corresponding above layer. The business layer contains the enterprise's business processes. The infrastructure service layer and the business service layer consist of services to ensure a linkage between the physical layers.

4.3.2 Building blocks in the SOA layer model

In Detecon's SOA layer model, ABBs can relate to the application layer or to the infrastructure layer. Both layers and their relations to other layers are shown more detailed in the following paragraphs.

Figure 13 shows in detail how ABBs in the application layer use infrastructure services and add own functionality to offer one or more building block services. Business services are designed on the basis of one or more building block services and they are used by business processes. Analogous, ABBs in the infrastructure layer offer one or

---

[162] cf. Lankes/Matthes/Wittenburg: Architekturmanagement 2005, p. 314 f.
[163] cf. Sebis: EA Tool Survey 2005, p. 24

more building block services. Infrastructure services are designed on the basis of one or more building block services and they are used by ABBs in the application layer, which can be seen in figure 14.

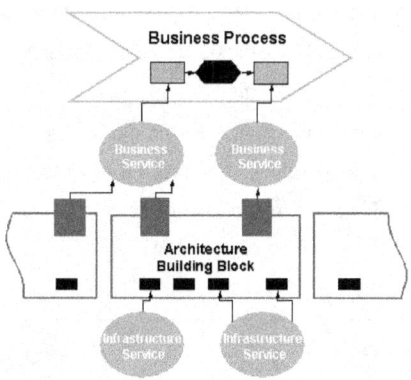

Figure 13: Detailed view on an ABB in the application layer[164]

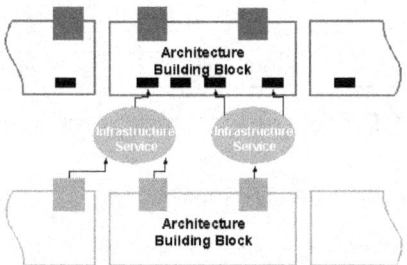

Figure 14: Detailed view on an ABB in the infrastructure layer[165]

In general, the life cycle of application building blocks is shorter than the life cycle of infrastructure building blocks. This can be validated by a simple example. Obviously, an infrastructure building block, providing a communication system (e.g. email), is used

---

[164] own figure, following Detecon: Service Oriented Enterprise Architecture 2006
[165] own figure, following Detecon: Service Oriented Enterprise Architecture 2006

for a much longer period of time, than an application building block, which supports a single product with a limited product life cycle. The number of infrastructure building blocks is lower than the number of application building blocks, which is caused by the fact that their services provided are more general. Especially short-term application building blocks are implemented to support a very special functionality. In contrast an infrastructure service, like database access, can be used equally across the enterprise's different lines of business. This also implies a higher occurrence of reuse. To ensure a consistent foundation for controlling, an exact definition of possible relationships has to be given. The limitation of the number of connections between building blocks and services is shown in table 1 and it can also be found in appendix A, modeled using UML.

Actor			Min	Max	
1	building block	offers	1	n	building block services
1	building block service	can be used by	0	n	infrastructure services/ business services
1	infrastructure service/ business service	uses	1	n	building block services
1	business building block	uses	1	n	infrastructure services
1	business process	uses	1	n	business services

Table 1: Relations between building block and services

4.3.3 Controlling the SOA layer model

When introducing IT controlling, a differentiation between the IT supply side and the IT demand side has been made. It has been mentioned that a cost allocation method has to consider both sides to transfer costs of IT provision to the users of IT services. In this model, business services build the linkage between IT supply side and IT demand side.

The SOA layer model builds a vertical linkage from the enterprise's infrastructure platform up to its business processes. Therefore, it provides a good basis to increase transparency of costs by developing a method to allocate and to distribute costs between the ABBs, services and business processes. While architectural layers are horizontal, IT controlling activities are conducted vertically across layers, affecting multiple layers.[166] Consequently, costs have to be charged bottom-up across the SOA layers as shown in figure 15.

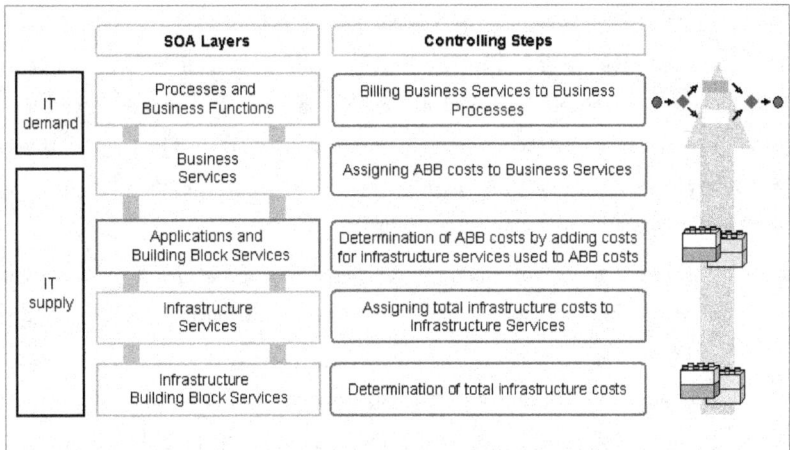

Figure 15: Controlling the SOA layer model[167]

The process of cost allocation consists of several steps, which are described shortly in the following:

- The costs for each ABB in the infrastructure layer have to be determined. The enterprise's total infrastructure costs equal the sum of all ABB costs.
- The costs of each ABB have to be distributed between its building block services.
- Infrastructure service costs can be calculated by aggregating costs for building block services used.
- The costs for an ABB in the application layer can be determined by adding costs for infrastructure service use to the ABB's costs.
- Again, costs of each ABB have to be distributed between its building block

---

[166] cf. Lankes/Matthes/Wittenburg: Architekturmanagement 2005, p. 315
[167] own figure

services.

- Again, costs of business services can be calculated by aggregating costs for building block services used.
- Business services are charged to business processes.

Obviously, there are activities that are conducted twice. This results from the analogies between the infrastructure layer and the application layer. Both consist of a set of building blocks, which provide building block services that are used by the respectively above layer. Therefore, the detailed description can be limited to three steps. Each of them has to be performed for both parts of the layer model:

- The determination of building block costs by using a life cycle model and differentiation between capital expenditures and operational expenditures (chapter 4.4).
- Allocation of ABB costs to its building block services (chapter 4.5).
- Definition of transfer prices that are used for cost allocation to users of infrastructure services and business services. Thus prospected use of services has to be planned (chapter 4.6).

4.3.4 Characterization of business processes

It is important to make a restriction regarding the type of business processes to be considered when allocating costs across the SOA layer model. This can be pointed out by an example from the insurance industry. Every enterprise has high volume and high-risk clients, which demand for individually designed contracts containing special terms and conditions, thus requiring particular attention. It would be wrong to charge every contract with the same costs, no matter its financial volume. A private client, small volume contract, would be charged the same amount like a multi-million corporate deal. While the second involves a high amount of manual contract design, the first is generated automatically.

Therefore it is assumed, that the cost allocation method does only cover business processes conducted without Business Intelligence (BI) support. These are mass processes, highly standardized and repeatable processes with relatively low financial volume. Excluded are high volume or high risk processes which are individually treated.

4.4 Determination of building block costs

4.4.1 Initial considerations

Enterprise Architecture Management with building blocks can be structured in Detecon's Business Enabling Approach. A life cycle cost model is needed for consistent valuation of building block management. A differentiation between initial investments and ongoing operational costs has to be made. Additionally, the investment decision for an ABB can be driven by a central instance in the enterprise or by a single LOB. Therefore, the IT value map is introduced to show coherences and resulting dependencies.

4.4.2 Detecon's Business Enabling Approach

As mentioned when introducing TOGAF, the TOGAF ADM is generic and has to be adapted to individual requirements to derive a tailored architecture development method. Detecon developed a TOGAF-based architecture management process, supporting strategic IT planning from business requirement management to budgeting, while integrating value management. Describing this process would go beyond the scope of this work. For the interested reader, the case study containing the complete process and a short description is available online.[168] In this book, a simplified process is used.

Figure 16 shows how business requirements are identified on the basis of business processes and how they are implemented as building blocks. Every single building block supports one or more business activities or respectively the appending business processes. Business requirements emerge from the enterprise's strategy and they are modeled in business processes. In a next step, correspondent ABBs are identified. Building Block Management has to ensure economic viability of the transformation of

---

[168] cf. Detecon: Strategic IT-Planning from Demand to Budget 2005

ABBs to SBBs by means of a make, buy or reuse decision. To support decision making of Building Block Management, a method to determine a building block costs is needed. The application of a life cycle model ensures to cover all related costs by analyzing the expenses in the single phases. The phases of the ABB life cycle correspond to classical life cycle models that have been applied to various IT assets (e.g. IT systems, applications, components).

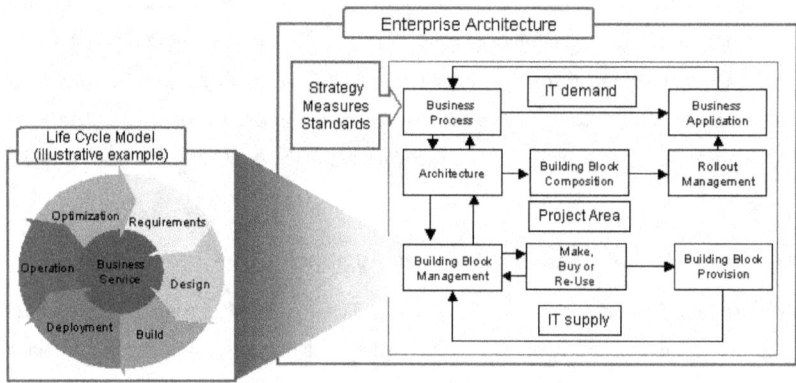

Figure 16: Detecon's Business Enabling Approach[169]

Unfortunately in practice, IT assets are rarely valuated covering their whole life cycle. Most enterprises focus on the determination of initial development costs, whereas ongoing operating expenses remain unconsidered.[170] IT controlling has to be in place from the very beginning to the very end to ensure economic efficiency.[171] Figure 16 shows the typical six phases of a life cycle and their sequence. The total life cycle costs of any asset can be calculated as the sum of costs of each phase in its life cycle.[172] To stay focused, the single phases are not described in detail because prospected readers are familiar with their contents and deliverables. Instead, the differences between Capital

---

[169] following Weber: Business Enabling Architecture 2002, p. 8, extended
[170] cf. Zarnekow/Brenner: Kosten im Lebenszyklus 2004, p. 338
[171] cf. Gadatsch: IT-Controlling 2005, p. 203 f.
[172] cf. Fischer: Kostencontrolling 2000, p. 268 f.

Expenditures (CAPEX) and Operational Expenditures (OPEX) are described.

4.4.3 Capital Expenditures versus Operational Expenditures

Capital Expenditures (CAPEX) are costs for initial capital investments, whereas Operational Expenditures (OPEX) are generated while keeping the enterprise running. Referring to the life cycle of an IT asset, CAPEX relate to the early phases, while OPEX emerge throughout the lifecycle. In general, when analyzing an enterprise's IT cost structure, OPEX is higher than CAPEX[173], which is a severe problem for many enterprises. A large part of the IT budget is used to keep IT running, while only a small part can be used to implement new functionality, which is needed to support emerging business requirements and innovations. The situation will get worse with IT budgets freezing or indeed decreasing, which is predicted by recent studies.[174] With a constant amount of OPEX, the CAPEX/OPEX ratio changes and the absolute amount of CAPEX has to be scaled down. SOA promises to help solving this problem by promoting reuse of existing building blocks,[175] even though the adoption of SOA requires some major investments in the beginning.

The application of a life cycle cost model ensures that a building block's CAPEX and OPEX are taken into account. Thus, Building Block Management's make, buy or reuse decision is based on complete cost information. Additionally, full allocation of life cycle costs to the IT demand side is ensured.

4.4.4 Building block budgeting

The argumentation for taking into account total life cycle costs can be equally transferred to building block budget calculation. Figure 17 shows the building block budgeting process of an example ABB from the Finance & Controlling domain and the correspondent SBB, taking into account CAPEX and OPEX.

---

[173] cf. Gerick: IT-Controlling 2003, p. 2
[174] cf. Capgemini: IT Trends 2006, p. 10
[175] cf. Pulier/Taylor: Enterprise SOA 2006, p. 51 f.

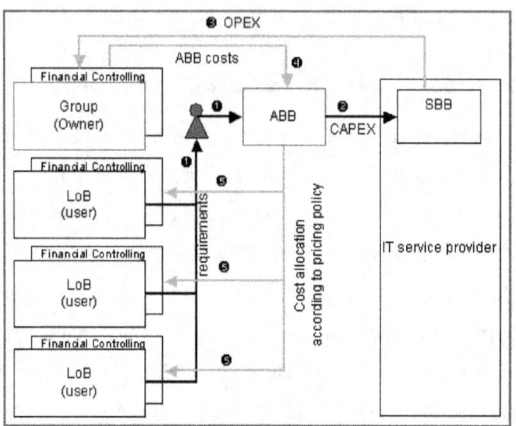

Figure 17: Building block budgeting[176]

The building block budgeting process consists of the following steps:

1. The ABB owner collects user requirements and specifies ABB functionality.
2. ABB owner calculates CAPEX to pay the IT service provider for implementation of the corresponding SBB.
3. IT service provider prices operation of the SBB. ABB owner calculates OPEX of the ABB.
4. Owner calculates the ABB's periodical costs, including CAPEX and OPEX, in order to allocate them to all users.
5. Transfer prices are defined on the basis of pricing policy applied. ABB users limit planning to allocated costs.

The IT service provider can either be enterprise-internal or an external partner. For the IT service provider, each SBB is an implementation project based on the requirements defined in the ABB. Therefore, CAPEX and OPEX are planned as a project.

---

[176] cf. Detecon: Service Oriented Enterprise Architecture 2006

4.4.5 IT value map

The IT value map is a method to structure IT investments regarding their value contribution to the group and their value contribution to a certain group member. It helps identifying, where specialization is beneficial and what segments should be standardized. Additionally, it helps showing the coherences and dependencies between investment decisions made by the group and the single LOBs.

The Chief Information Officer (CIO), who is in charge of central management of all IT activities, represents the group. With IT getting more and more important, the CIO's tasks become increasingly management related.[177] Today, the CIO is responsible for IT governance in the majority of enterprises and he or she is assessed by the business value created by IT.[178] Some CIOs delegate supervision of technical areas to a Chief Technology Officer (CTO).[179] Therefore in the following, the group is represented by the CIO/CTO. These central management offices do not produce any products that generate income or profit. But there are CIO/CTO-driven investments. Central IT infrastructures support global processes and knowledge sharing.[180] Thus, they are beneficial to all group members. An enterprise-wide implementation has to be organized by a central organizational unit. Hence, the CIO/CTO office is the owner of the relevant building block. A major infrastructure investment, which yields profit for many departments, involves high fixed costs. CIO/CTO-driven infrastructure investments are referred to as corporate investments. If financed by the CIO/CTO office, its costs have to be shared across the enterprise to discharge the budget.[181] Therefore, costs for expensive corporate investments have to be taken into account when allocating costs. Though, the CTO office has to promote and control the use of infrastructure investments in order to prevent redundancies. On the other hand, investments can be driven by a single LOB. In spite of all consolidation activities, there will be different

---

[177] cf. Michels/Pölzl: CIO 2002, p. 3
[178] cf. Weill/Ross: IT Governance 2004, p. 227 ff.
[179] In practice the CTO is ranked in different hierarchical levels, equal or reporting to the CIO. In either case, the CTO's tasks are more technically, including responsibility for the development of IT infrastructure.
[180] cf. Ross/Rockart: Reconceptualizing IT 1999, p. 9 f.
[181] cf. Ross/Vitale/Beath: IT chargeback 1998, p. 3

requirements, which cannot be fulfilled completely by the central infrastructure, for instance a special Customer Relationship Management (CRM) system for individual product services, which is useless for other LOBs. Therefore, implementation will be driven by the respective LOB and ownership will be located in the LOB.

The concept of the IT value map can be best explained by an example, which is also the basis for figure 18:

> Deutsche Telekom group offers services to clients on the basis of different network technologies (Internet, mobile phone networks, etc.). Each LOB is focused on one network technology, e.g. T-Online offers online services (e.g. via DSL), T-Mobile offers mobile services.

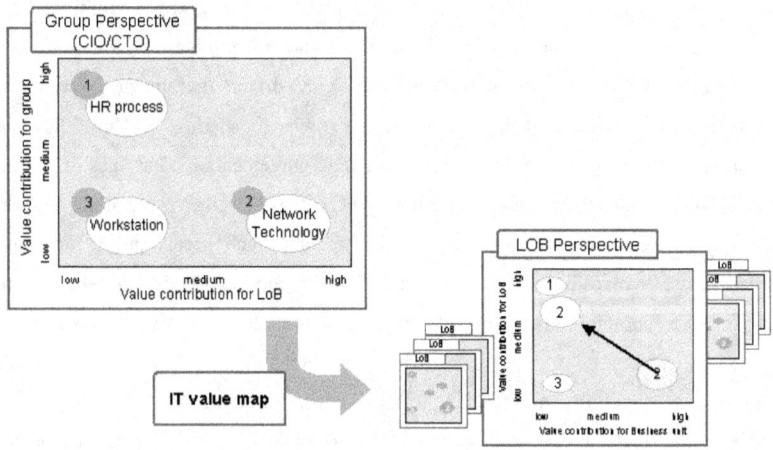

Figure 18: IT value map[182]

Analyzing the three example items in the IT value map shows the different positions and how they change when the view is shifted from the group (left side) to a single LOB (right side):

---

[182] own figure, following Detecon: Service Oriented Enterprise Architecture 2006

- Human Resources (HR) processes:
  Enterprise-wide optimization of HR processes can offer a high value contribution to the group, by offering better recruiting or training. A specialized HR process in a single LOB will not generate additional value. The same argumentation holds when shifting the view to a single LOB.

- Network technologies:
  Specializing the network technology within a single LOB to support the services offered provides a high value contribution and it can generate a competitive advantage. Shifting the view to a single LOB, the network technology is standardized for all business units and a further specialization is not valuable. Therefore the position changes.

- Workstations:
  Optimization of workstations does not offer a high value contribution, neither to the group nor to a single LOB, because it does not provide an advantage at the market.

The IT value map shows that investment decisions made on enterprise level influence the group's LOBs. Costs, which emerge from the decision to implement a standardized solution on enterprise-level, have to be allocated to all LOBs. Consequently, besides the distinction made between CAPEX and OPEX, costs can be structured regarding the origin of cost, which can be the CIO/CTO office or the LOB.

4.4.6 The cost element matrix

When determining costs, in a first step cost categories that adhere to the resources used have to be defined.[183] Examples for commonly used cost categories for the IT domain are hardware, software, peripherals, human resources, and external services.[184] As this work cannot provide a detailed set of cost categories that is applicable to each and every enterprise, it provides some very general examples of groups of cost elements that relate to the building block approach. However, they include the cost categories mentioned.

---

[183] cf. Wöhe: Allgemeine Betriebswitschaftslehre 2002, p. 1088
[184] cf. Michels: IT-Betriebsabrechnung 2004, p. 6

Knowing that costs can emerge from CIO/CTO investments, which are corporate investments, as well as from a LOB investments, including both CAPEX and OPEX, they can be structured regarding the two dimensions origin and type of costs as illustrated by the matrix in figure 19.

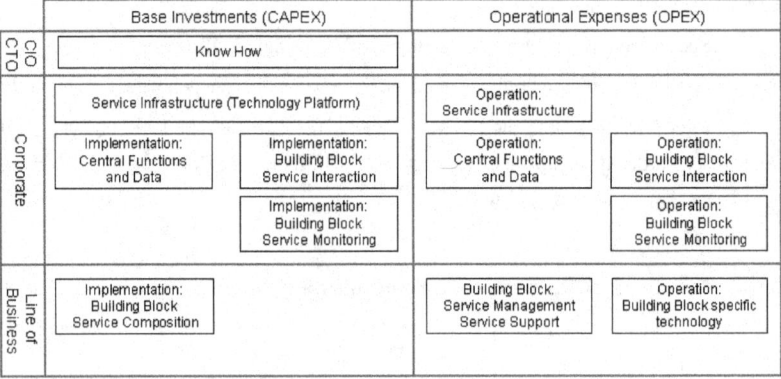

Figure 19: Cost element matrix[185]

A good example for costs emerging from the CIO/CTO office relate to the generation of know how. After the decision to adopt SOA has been made, the CIO/CTO office starts research in order to select the appropriate technology platform and to implement the service infrastructure. Therefore, the service infrastructure is a CIO/CTO-driven investment, which generates a large sum of operational costs. Central functions and data, building block service interaction and building block monitoring are other examples for common corporate investments. In fact, all enterprise-wide integration functions are corporate investments, and they also generate operational expenses. The implementation of an LOB-specific building block will result in implementation costs and it will generate operational expenses for service support and building block specific technology.

---

[185] own figure

4.4.7 Implications for controlling

As we have seen, to determine an ABB's costs, CAPEX and OPEX have to be assessed throughout the life cycle, taking into account costs for CIO/CTO-driven corporate investments. CIO/CTO costs have to be shared by all LOBs in the group, whereas costs emerging LOB-internal are shared by corresponding building blocks. The life cycle model to determine direct costs has to be applied to every single ABB in the business layer and the infrastructure layer.

When determining cost of an ABB in the application layer, usage of infrastructure services has to be considered. By applying the introduced process of vertical cost allocation across the architectural layers in the SOA layer model, infrastructure costs are transferred to applications by usage of infrastructure services.

4.5 Pricing of building block services

A building block's functionality can be accessed through building block services. Therefore, they provide a possibility to transfer costs to its users. Consistent costing and pricing of building block services is critical to success of controlling model adoption. Basically, building block costs have to be shared amongst its building block services. Depending on the individual cost share ratio, a certain proportion of costs is allocated to each building block service. In the following, determination of cost share ratios for building block services is referred to as

"pricing policy for building block services".

In a first step, costs are determined and adjacently, prices are defined, which can vary from calculated costs. The transfer price charged results in costs in the respectively above layer. After shifting the view to the above layer, the amount cannot be influenced anymore.

There are two aspects to consider when choosing pricing policies. First, the more detailed the design of cost share ratios and thus the process of determination, the higher the effort and costs caused. Pricing policies can be chosen differently between the Application layer and the Infrastructure layer. Actually a different pricing policy may be applied to every single building block. Second, the level of cost recovery can be controlled. When organized as a cost center, the objective is total cost recovery, whereas a profit center has to add a margin. Profit centers can be organized in several ways, for instance, as enterprise-internal subsystems, making autonomous decisions with success responsibility (also on external markets), or like cost centers, adding a margin to costs for internal transfer prices.[186] To keep the argumentation simple, all examples given in this book apply a cost center approach to achieve full cost recovery, which is also common corporate practice.[187] In addition, costs are shared proportionally. Policies can be replaced by more sophisticated cost share ratios or a profit center approach. Therefore, they are referred to as pricing policies and the amount charged is called transfer price. When applying a cost center approach, the sum of share ratios has to be one, whereas a profit center has to adjust share ratios to internal or external market prices. The assumption of a profit margin would result in higher share ratios, leading to a sum greater than one.

To ensure full cost recovery, building block costs have to be shared amongst the building block services used. The problem of assigning costs to unused building block services can be explained by a typical example, which can be found alike in many enterprises:

> In the given architectural environment, a SAP system, or respectively one SAP module, is seen as one building block that offers several building block services. In practice, an enterprise rarely uses all building block services provided.

Possible policies for building block service pricing:

- Proportional allocation:
  The argument for a proportional allocation of building block costs to all building block services provided is that they cause these costs by their existence even if they are not used. The drawback of this alternative is that the part of costs allocated to unused services is not transferred to the business units and thus, it still charges the owner's budget.

---

[186] cf. Voß/Gutenschwager: Informationsmanagement 2001, p. 100
[187] cf. Ewert/Wagenhofer: Interne Unternehmensrechnung 2005, p. 640

- Proportional allocation, limited to building block services used:
  The limitation of building block services provides the solution to the drawback of the previous alternative. Costs of used building block services will be higher, sharing the part of costs previously allocated to unused building block services.

According to the motivated purposes of the controlling model, the second alternative is the better solution. There are two suggestive arguments for this decision. Regarding the motivation of increased cost awareness, it is important to charge all costs that emerge from the existence of an IT solution. If a business requirement is supported by an oversized solution, like the exemplary SAP system, all costs have to be charged to the enterprise's business units to show real costs caused by these entities. A building block with a large part of unused functionality is a candidate for a cost saving analysis. When analyzing the possibility of replacing an existing system, only functionality needed will be developed or procured, while costs must be compared to full ABB costs.

4.6 Pricing of business services and infrastructure services

4.6.1 The concept of virtual services

The infrastructure service layer and the business service layer are based on the concept of virtual services to ensure a linkage between the physical layers. So first, the idea of virtualization has to be explained and second, it has to be shown how it is applied in the SOA layer model.

'*Virtualization*' is a very general term that refers to the abstraction of physical resources across many aspects of IT to hide complexity or integrate functionality.[188] How virtualization is used in the SOA layer model can be explained by focusing on one of the two appearances. The business service layer is chosen, as it is more comprehensible to the majority of readers and it is prevalent to the business side of the enterprise. The explanation can be transferred to the infrastructure service layer.

When modeled as an Event-driven Process Chain (EPC), a business process in its

---

[188] cf. Figueiredo/Dinda/Fortes: Virtualization 2005, p. 28

minimalist specification consists of business functions initiated by events.[189] The application layer consists of a set of building blocks. The building blocks provide building block services. A business function is business-oriented and normally it uses more than one building block service. *'Virtual services'* are designed to build the linkage between both architectural layers by integrating all building block services, required by a business function as one business service.[190] Virtual services meet the principles of service orientation as introduced in chapter 1.2.2.

4.6.2 Using virtual services for controlling

As the linkage between application layer and business layer, virtual services are the unit used to allocate costs. Having defined the possible relations between building block services and business services[191] in this way allows for calculation of business service costs. Again a pricing policy has to be defined. The building block service price has to be shared amongst the using business services. Depending on the individual share ratio, a certain proportion of the building block service price is allocated to each business service. Consequently, business services aggregate a portion of the price of every building block service used. Again, share ratios can influence the distribution of costs and the level of cost recovery. In the following, determination of cost share ratios for business services is referred to as

"*pricing policy for building block service reuse*".

Obviously, a higher occurrence of reuse results in smaller share ratios, leading to smaller proportions of building block service prices and finally, to lower business service prices. Due to the characteristics of the business service layer and the infrastructure layer, in general, a cost center approach can be assumed. The functionality provided by building block services is recomposed without adding any functionality. There may be costs for service composition, which in case have to be added to the service price.

---

[189] cf. Keller/Nüttgens/Scheer: EPK Modellierung 1992, p. 7 f.
[190] cf. Erl: Service-Oriented Architecture 2005, p. 333 f.
It may be helpful to have a look at figure 13 or respectively figure 14 to avoid confusion of terms.
[191] cf. table 1 or appendix A

4.7 Controlling IT demand

4.7.1 Planning costs and cost allocation

The last step of cost allocation across the SOA layer model is transferring IT costs to the enterprise's business units, which have been defined as the IT demand side. Business services build the linkage between IT and the enterprise's business processes. From the business process view, business service prices result in IT costs. After the determination of business service costs, the prospected usage of services has to be planned in order to define the service price per reuse that can be charged to business processes. Additionally, analysis of service usage allows for activities to promote reuse. As previously mentioned, higher occurrences of reuse result in lower costs per reuse. Consequently both domains, but especially business, benefit from more frequent reuse. Figure 20 shows the sequence of service costing, usage planning, service pricing, and enterprise-internal marketing.

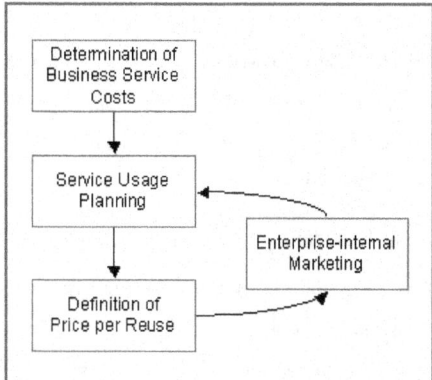

Figure 20: Business service - planning, costing, pricing[192]

---

[192] own figure

4.7.2 Service usage planning and enterprise-internal marketing

Actual reuse has to be determined in order to calculate the price per reuse. Additionally, future usage has to be planned. Therefore, the analysis of business service usage has to provide answers to the following questions:

- Which business processes use a certain service?
- Which business processes can be supported, but currently do not use the service?
- Which potential future business processes will use the service?

Actual usage data shows in how many business processes a service is used. Analyzing appropriateness of business services to support other business processes can identify additional reuse potentials. Reuse potentials should already be considered in building block design. Using a certain business service can be promoted by communicating cost saving potentials emerging from a lower price per reuse. Useful planning periods can be for instance two year and five year forecasts.

Promoting reuse is beneficial for the enterprise, but also for building block owners and reusing units. Higher reuse leads to more efficient usage of IT resources throughout the enterprise. A business unit, that owns a building block and uses it exclusively, has to bear all costs itself. A potential second user would share costs and thus decrease the business unit's IT costs. For the second user in general, a reuse solution will be less expensive than an individual solution.

4.7.3 Business service pricing

Business services provide the linkage between business processes, which belong to the business domain, and business services, which belong to the IT domain. As they are used to transfer costs from the IT supply side to the IT demand side, business service pricing is the most sophisticated part of the cost allocation process.

Having determined building block costs and business service costs, is a large step towards realizing the purposes of the controlling model, which are increased cost transparency and increased cost awareness. But charging of IT costs can also have drawbacks, which mainly emerge from acceptance problems. Undesirable outcomes of cost allocation via IT service prices can be endless complaints, lack of trust, and averting for formal processes, which can lead to the rejection of use of shared services.[193] To avoid them, results of cost determination, the cost allocation mechanisms, and pricing policies have to be made transparent and comprehensively communicated.

ROSS/VITALE/BEATH (1999) developed an IT chargeback model, which illustrates the function of IT charges.[194] Accordingly, IT charges are determined by chargeback policies and administrative practices, and they are the basis for decision making and performance evaluations. Besides potential benefits in corporate performance, the authors motivate perceived fairness in business units. Figure 21 shows an adapted version that has been modified to fit in the given architectural environment and the structure of this book.

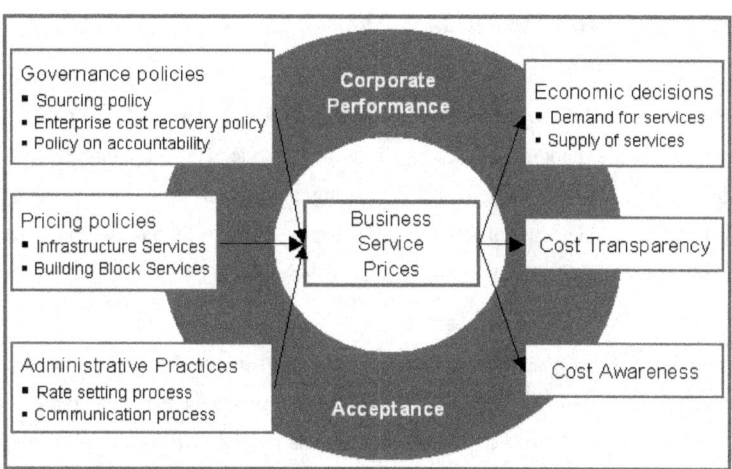

Figure 21: Defining IT service prices[195]

An enterprise's sourcing policy determines whether business units can obtain IT services from an external IT service provider or if they are limited to internal service

---
[193] cf. Weill/Ross: IT Governance 2004, p. 227 ff.
[194] cf. Ross/Vitale/Beath: IT chargeback 1999, p. 19
[195] own figure, following Ross/Vitale/Beath: IT chargeback 1999, p. 19, extended

provision. The cost recovery policy determines if IT service provision is organized as a cost center or as a profit center. The cost allocation policy regulates the accountability for IT charges by defining the responsibilities for IT investment and IT usage decisions. Additionally, the chosen pricing policies for building block services and infrastructure services influence business service pricing. The definition of administrative practices increases transparency for all parties involved. The process of rate setting has to be described and communicated comprehensively. Balanced definition of policies will result in widely accepted business service prices, which increase cost transparency, promote cost awareness, and support economic decision making in order to achieve a higher corporate performance.

4.8 Controlling model overview

4.8.1 Summarizing the model

Obviously, there are many possibilities to adjust cost allocation to an enterprise's specific needs. A high freedom of choice creates potential for strategic control. The price of a single building block, building block service, infrastructure service, or business service can be modified by choosing a different combination of pricing policies. This enables enterprise-internal sponsoring of IT solutions, certain business activities, single products, or a whole LOB. The definition of enterprise specific pricing policies is a part of IT governance.

To avoid acceptance problems, it may be beneficial to start with cost-oriented pricing policies, which is common practice.[196] This is the first step to increase cost transparency and cost awareness. In a next step, policies can be refined and market price oriented policies may be adopted. It can be beneficial to limit the implementation of market mechanisms to parts of the enterprise.[197] With the given controlling model, they can be realized for a limited set of business units or for reuse of a specific building block or service. Hence choosing a set of pricing policies is not a one-off decision, but policies have to be revised continually.

---

[196] cf. Kaplan/Atkinson: Advanced Management Accounting 1998, p. 458
[197] cf. Ewert/Wagenhofer: Interne Unternehmensrechnung 2005, p. 618 ff.

Controlling model development   81

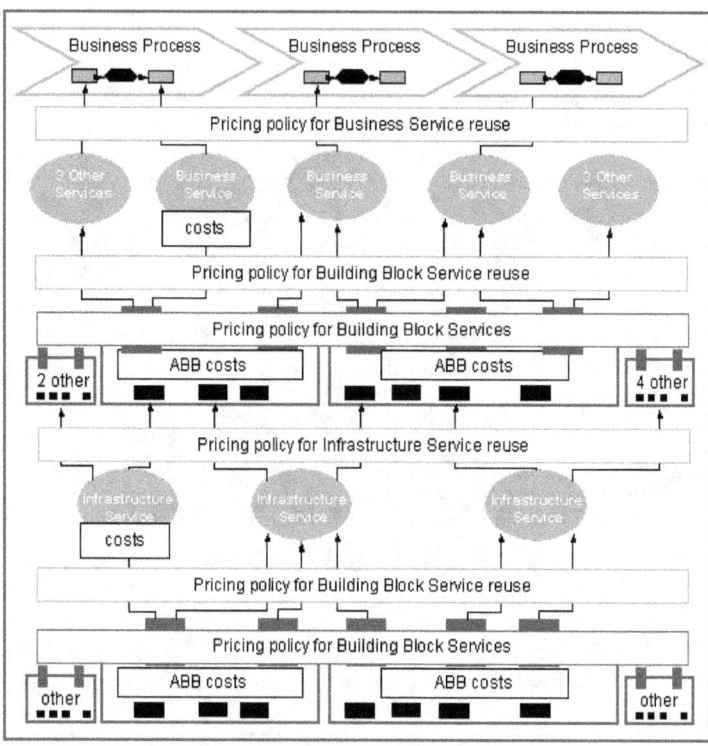

Figure 22: Controlling model overview[198]

4.8.2 Calculation example

Figure 23 shows a calculation example with assumed figures. It can be seen how costs are aggregated and distributed when adopting a certain set of pricing policies. To limit complexity, the infrastructure layer and business processes are blinded out and analysis is focused on two building blocks and three business services, while a group of others shows that there are more. With the simplest possible choice, all pricing policies allocate costs proportionally to the respective user. Thereby, cost transparency and cost awareness are increased with a minimum of effort.

---

[198] own figure

From a bottom-up perspective, Infrastructure Service costs are distributed proportionally to reusing ABBs in the application layer. Total ABB costs in the application layer can be calculated by adding costs for service reuse to ABB costs.

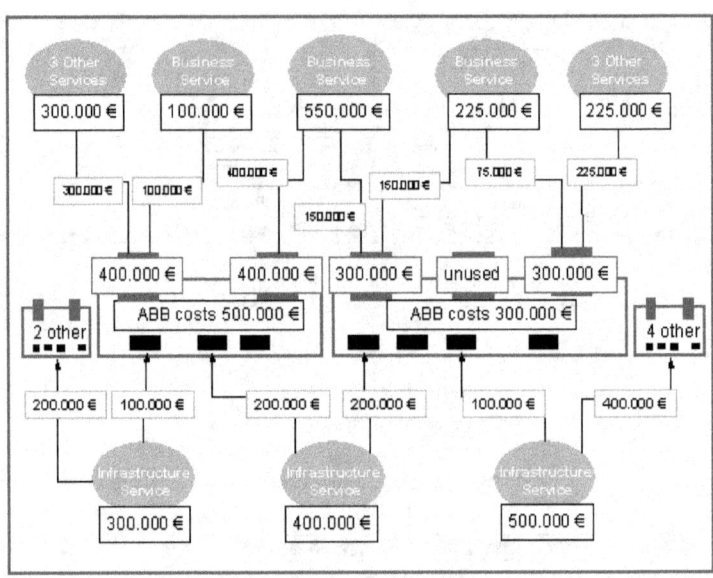

Figure 23: Calculation example[199]

Calculation for the left ABB: building block costs   500.000 €
                                infrastructure service usage   300.000 €
                                total   800.000 €

Building block costs are distributed proportionally among building block services, which are used by business services. Unused building block services cannot be used to transfer costs to business units. Building block service costs are distributed proportionally to reusing business services. Business service costs can be calculated by summarizing the partial costs for building block services used.

---

[199] own figure

4.9 Controlling maturity model

The adoption of SOA is not a one-off project, and neither is the implementation of the developed controlling model. Financial controlling has to be adequate for the Enterprise Architecture and its actual granularity. Therefore, a stepwise adoption of SOA must include adjustment and refinement of financial controlling.

The maturity model (figure 24) provides a roadmap for implementing the controlling model and it shows the enterprise's actual situation. In the worst case (level 1), IT costs are managed as one cost block. At level 2, IT costs can be allocated to domains. At level 3, cost information is available for single platforms or applications. To reach level 4, the developed controlling model has to be used to allocate costs to building blocks and business services. With every level, granularity of financial analysis is refined. Thereby, accuracy of financial figures is increased, which allows for calculation of more precise controlling figures. This increases specificity and improves quality of decision making.

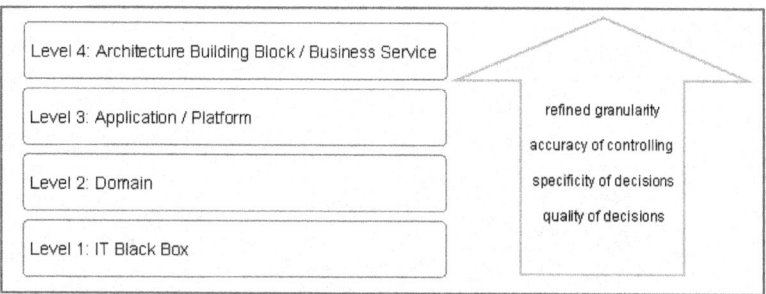

Figure 24: Controlling maturity model[200]

The single levels are geared to the hierarchical system of planning objects (figure 8). Therefore, granularity of actually available financial data can also be visualized in the corresponding figure.

---

[200] own figure

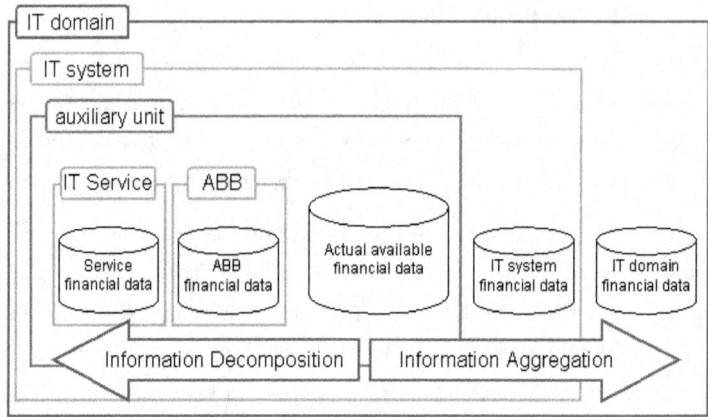

Figure 25: Controlling maturity visualized[201]

---

[201] own figure

5 Controlling model application

5.1 IT supply side

The cost information provided by the developed controlling model can be used on the IT supply side to improve IT provision. Consistent financial information allows for optimization of the enterprise's portfolio of building blocks and its portfolio of services through application of favored controlling methods. The decision maker is not forced to apply a certain method. It enables calculation of performance indicators and thus, it provides a basis for internal and external benchmarking.[202] Additionally, the controlling model data enables investment valuation for single building blocks. In both cases granularity of analysis can be adapted to the needs of the object of investigation.

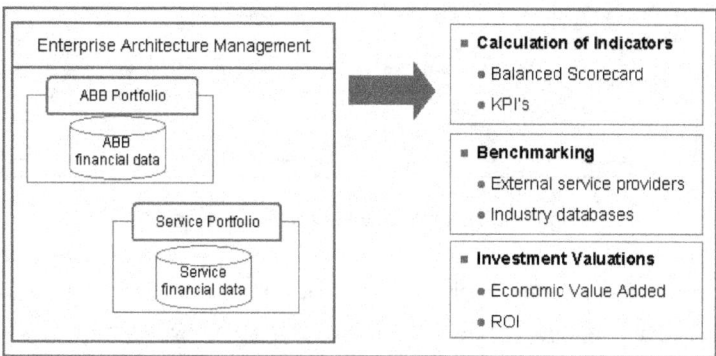

Figure 26: Enabling controlling of IT supply[203]

The cost information provided can also be used for reporting purposes. Data can be aggregated and financial figures can be structured in order to match the CEO and CFO perspective.

---

[202] cf. Burger: Kostenmanagement 1999, p. 106 ff.
[203] own figure

5.2 IT demand side

Referring to the definition given for IT Performance Management, activities are not limited to IT supply, but they have to cover both sides.[204] Cost information provided by the developed controlling model can also be used on the IT demand side, which are the enterprise's business units. The existence of transfer prices results in more elaborated decisions on IT usage.[205]

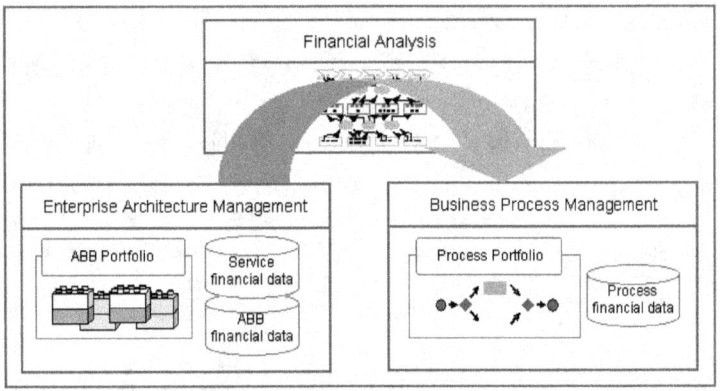

Figure 27: Enabling Activity Based Costing[206]

Figure 27 shows how the developed controlling model provides the data needed in business units. In the given SOA layer model, business processes use business services that directly support their business functions. The controlling model ensures the linkage of IT costs to business processes by allocating costs to business services.

Conventional company cost accounting systems are not suitable to deliver cost information the way it is needed by decision makers.[207] Business activities can be modeled in business processes. The application of Activity Based Costing (ABC) is an appropriate instrument for financial controlling of processes and it opens up various

---
[204] cf. Kütz: Kennzahlen der IT 2003, p. 139 f.
[205] cf. Ewert/Wagenhofer: Interne Unternehmensrechnung 2005, p. 626 f.
[206] own figure
[207] cf. Braun: Prozeßkostenrechnung 1994, p. 9

new possibilities for analysis. Instead of measuring inputs, ABC focuses on the costs of outputs.[208] Therefore, it fosters the understanding of costs of business processes as motivated in the introductory chapter by providing comprehensible units. The majority of business processes is supported by IT or strongly dependent on IT. Thus, IT costs have to be taken into account for evaluation of business processes and performance assessment.

Business units can optimize their process portfolio on the basis of the cost information provided. Regarding business processes and business services, the following list of questions, which does not claim to be complete, can be answered with the controlling model in place:

- Questions concerning a business service:
  - Which are the main cost drivers (which process is the main user of this service)?
  - How many processes use the service?
  - How much does the service cost?
  - How much does the service cost, if it is externally procured?
- Questions concerning a business process:
  - How much does the process cost?
  - How many services does the process use?
  - Which services does the process use?
  - Are services used exclusively?
  - Which are the services that mainly determine the overall process cost?

Summarizing, ABC is the appropriate instrument for the financial valuation of processes and the developed controlling model provides the input cost data needed to integrate IT costs in ABC.

---

[208] cf. Granof/Platt/Vaysman: Activity-Based Costing 2000, p. 7

5.3 Sourcing decisions and legacy system valuation

5.3.1 Outsourcing

The term outsourcing is a combination of the words outside and resourcing. Early forms of outsourcing emerged from the external provision of IT hardware.[209] In general, outsourcing can affect different functions in an enterprise but in the following, the scope is limited to IT. Therefore, '*outsourcing*' can be defined as

"... *handing over IT tasks to the responsibility of a different company, ...* "[210]

which also implies that IT assets, needed to perform the respective tasks, are no longer located in the enterprise. Therefore, the argumentation from an enterprise's view can also be the other way around. An IT asset is subject to outsourcing, thus the tasks conducted are handed over to an external company.

Outsourcing has to be seen in distinction to a make-or-buy decision, concerning a single IT asset, for instance software application development.[211] Possible IT assets for outsourcing can be a hardware system, network infrastructure, desktops, but also service functions such as IT user help desk or a complete IT department.[212] Granularity can be chosen depending on the specific purpose. Outsourcing large parts of an enterprise's IT is a strategic decision because it cannot be reversed or revised in the short term.[213] With SOA, granularity can be chosen as small as a single service. The abstraction of business functionality from the physical implementation facilitates replacement of a building block. Service functionality, quality, and design are described in SLAs, which provide a basis for comparison of service providers[214] and they allow for replacement of services without affecting the entire application or infrastructure.

Service outsourcing can be organized in two ways. Either an Application Service Provider (ASP) hosts a service in a physically separated IT system, or the provider

---

[209] cf. Dittrich/Braun: Business Process Outsourcing 2004, p. 3
[210] cf. Krcmar: Informationsmanagement 2005, p. 371
[211] cf. Hauer/Settele: IV-Controlling durch Outsourcing 2000, p. 180
[212] cf. Voß/Gutenschwager: Informationsmanagement 2001, p. 103
[213] cf. Horváth: Controlling 2004, p. 740
[214] cf. Weill/Ross: IT Governance 2004, p. 101

operates a service in the client's IT system (in house hosting), which also includes the personnel needed.[215]

In his widely debated article "IT doesn't matter", CARR (2003) rated IT as a commodity article and stated, that the use of information technology cannot provide a competitive advantage and thus has no strategic importance.[216] This is an argument for outsourcing an enterprise's IT. In contrast, analysts found out, that after many cost-driven outsourcing deals, enterprises start to analyze how outsourcing and IT can contribute business value.[217] It can also be a strategic option to access knowledge or a certain technology. In this case, IT is the enabler for new business activities or it fosters efficiency of IT support for actual business.

The main drivers for outsourcing are cost savings, reduced risks, and personnel savings.[218] As a profit center organization in a competitive market, outsourcing providers are forced to operate efficiently and to offer market prices.[219] Besides expected cost reductions, other financial outcomes are increased cost control and more variable IT costs. Additionally, outsourcing of standardized processes allows for concentration on core competencies. However, there are risks additional to fall short of one's expectations. Outsourcing can lead to strong dependencies, a loss of operative control, or a loss of competencies (including personnel), and security problems can occur.[220] Therefore, outsourcing is not appropriate for IT systems with strategic relevance and core competencies.[221]

The outsourcing industry promotes SOA as the enabler for the industrialization of IT, forecasting that services are produced on a mass scale and implemented in an assembly-line fashion.[222] However, SOA allows for flexible sourcing decisions and outsourcing is only one of many sourcing options. Especially for large enterprises, there are several ways to organize IT supply and outsourcing projects should be examined carefully.

---

[215] cf. Masak: Enterprise Architekturen 2005, p. 14
[216] cf. Carr: IT doesn't matter 2003, 41 ff.
[217] cf. Gartner: Outsourcing 2005, p. 4
[218] cf. Horváth: Controlling 2004, p. 740
[219] cf. Hauer/Settele: IV-Controlling durch Outsourcing 2000, p. 185
[220] cf. Hauer/Settele: IV-Controlling durch Outsourcing 2000, p. 180 f.
[221] cf. Horváth: Controlling 2004, p. 740
[222] cf. Hurwitz: Industrialization 2005

Therefore, when motivating the benefits of SOA, the term sourcing was used, which implies that SOA improves outsourcing possibilities, but it also enables more flexible internal sourcing.

Besides others, possible sourcing options are:[223]

- Insourcing:
  All IT services are provided enterprise-internal, thus it is the opposite of outsourcing. In a large enterprise, all LOBs can obtain IT services from an internal IT service provider or distributed IT service providers share their offers.
- Cosourcing:
  Collaboration of enterprises that pool together identical IT services in order to reach the size and volume needed for economically efficient operation.
- Backsourcing
  The process of reintegrating previously outsourced IT services.

It has to be shown, that the developed controlling model can provide financial information to support efficient sourcing decisions. The cost information gained through application of the developed controlling model helps to calculate costs in order to compare different sourcing options.

5.3.2 Visualizing sourcing objects in the SOA layer model

In the controlling model, costs are allocated bottom-up across the architectural layers. Therefore, the SOA layer model can also be used to visualize possible sourcing objects. It provides a guideline for financial calculations. To support the argumentation, three possible sourcing objects (figure 28) have been chosen. They are explained in the following paragraphs.

A common task for Enterprise Architecture Management is a sourcing decision for a building block. Therefore, two possible situations are given to show how costs can be calculated and what issues have to be concerned. In type I the building block is located in the Infrastructure layer, whereas in type II it is part of the application layer. With

---

[223] cf. Hodel/Berger/Risi: Outsourcing 2004, p. 25 f.

Business Process Outsourcing (BPO) getting popular, type III shows how to calculate costs for a sourcing decision for a whole business process.

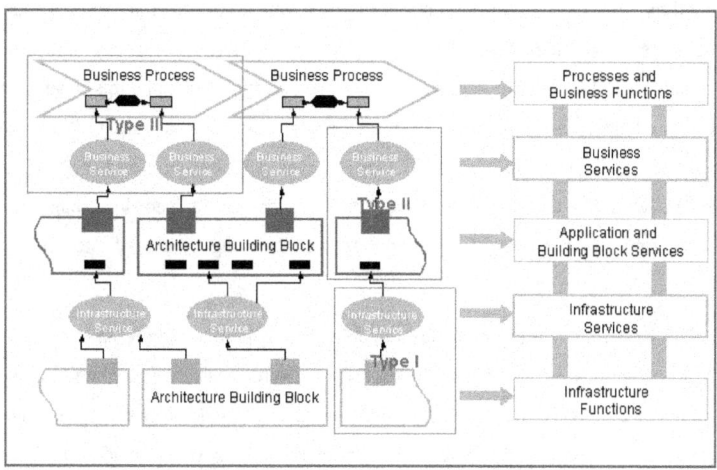

Figure 28: Possible sourcing objects[224]

5.3.3 Building block sourcing

Type I simulates a sourcing decision for a building block in the infrastructure layer. Having the possible relationships between building blocks, building block services, and infrastructure services in mind, several situations may occur. The building block provides building block services whose usage is limited to one infrastructure service. Given the developed cost allocation method, building block costs equal infrastructure service costs. Therefore, a possible sourcing decision has to be based on these costs. If the respective infrastructure service does not integrate other building block services, it may also be subject to a sourcing decision, instead of the underlying building block. If building block services are used by different infrastructure services, building block costs are the basis for the decision. Changing the sourcing strategy for an infrastructure

---

[224] own figure

service that is based on a building block, which also serves other infrastructure services, is much more sophisticated. It has to be analyzed which part of building block costs can be influenced. For instance, replacement of a single building block service, which is provided by a SAP system through a more individual solution, will not result in savings regarding building block costs. Parts, which are subject to outsourcing, can produce redundancies if they cannot replace a complete building block. In this case, a more sophisticated analysis is needed. Coming back to the SAP example, it has to be evaluated if replacement is beneficial. The Enterprise Architecture and the controlling model show dependencies to support more differentiated decision making. The argumentation can be analogously transferred to building blocks of the application layer.

A special case for sourcing of a building block is Type II in figure 28. If a building block in the application layer is based on infrastructure services, which are exclusively used, outsourcing the building block would result in unused infrastructure services or infrastructure building blocks. Thus, the costs of exclusively used services and building blocks in the layers beneath have to be taken into account.

5.3.4 Business Process (Out-)sourcing (BPO)

Despite the initial note, that the focus of the financial calculations in this chapter lies on IT assets, BPO is mentioned shortly, due to the practical relevance. The idea of BPO is that a third-party firm manages an entire business process, such as accounting, factoring, procurement, or human resources.[225] The external provider also takes on responsibility for the IT tasks included.[226]

Business processes are the users of business services and they share costs for a consolidated business service. Two possible situations may occur. If a business service has been exclusively used by the respective business process, it is not needed anymore after a BPO. The cost saving achieved depends on the reuse of underlying building blocks. If any building block is not needed anymore, a partial cost saving can be

---

[225] cf. Dittrich/Braun: Business Process Outsourcing 2004, p. 4 f.
[226] cf. Gadatsch/Mayer: IT-Controlling 2004, p. 203

realized. If the business service is shared with other business services, costs for the business service will remain constant. Its costs will be shared between a smaller group of business processes, thus resulting in higher costs per reuse.

The idea of BPO can also be transferred to enterprise-internal sourcing decisions. A group may decide to implement a central HR management. From a single LOB's view, the HR processes are relocated to a central unit and cost savings can be calculated as described above.

5.3.5 Legacy system valuation

The financial valuation of legacy systems follows the principles applied to support sourcing decisions. As shown in figure 29, a legacy system usually comprises a set of building blocks from the application layer and the infrastructure layer.

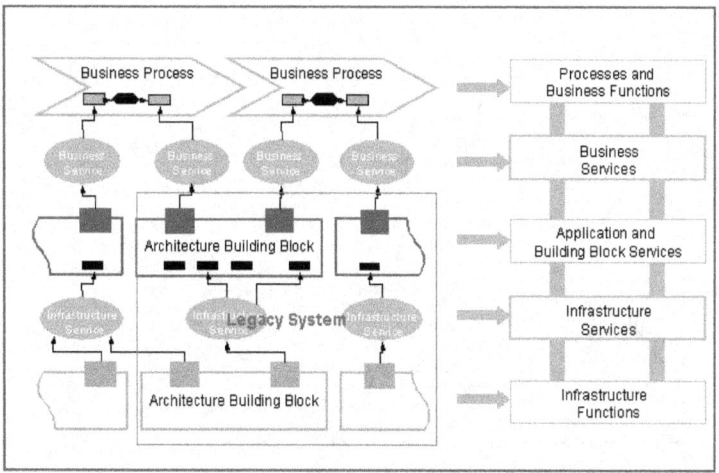

Figure 29: Legacy system valuation[227]

Business services are designed to integrate the legacy system and they build the linkage

---

[227] own figure

to business processes.[228] A good example is a monolithic mainframe system, which includes business applications and data storage. The evolutionary character of SOA allows for stepwise migration and it does not necessarily require replacement of existing solutions. Legacy systems can be integrated with service-oriented solutions using wrapper services, which offer the functionality provided.[229] When comparing costs of the legacy system to a possible solution for replacement, costs for support of the business functions provided have to be calculated. Consequently, application building blocks and infrastructure building blocks have to be taken into account. Normally, legacy systems are migrated stepwise. Therefore, continual revisions of economic efficiency of maintaining the legacy system is needed. The less functionality used, the higher are the costs allocated to building block services that are still in use. At a certain point in time, legacy system operation is no longer valuable.

5.3.6 Summarizing sourcing calculation support

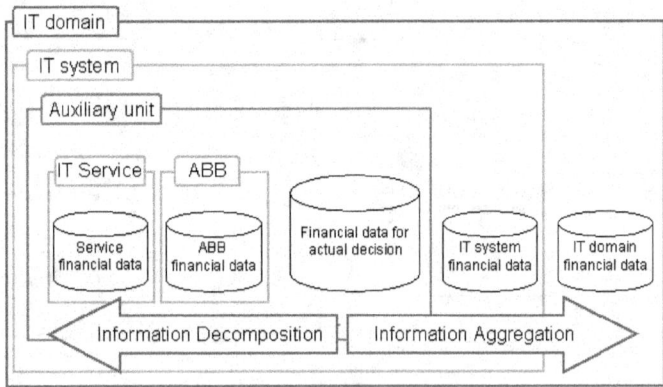

Figure 30: Information aggregation and decomposition[230]

In general to support a sourcing decision, the relevant costs of the respective group of

---
[228] cf. Erl: Service-Oriented Architecture 2005, p. 333 ff.
[229] cf. Masak: Enterprise Architekturen 2005, p. 222 f.
[230] own figure

elements to be sourced can be calculated by aggregating the corresponding cost information. The idea of information aggregation and decomposition can also be used for valuation of legacy systems. Obviously, the composite character of Enterprise Architecture and SOA is reflected. Inspired from the idea of flexible composition of applications and business processes, this method offers a possibility to complete the solutions constructed with financial data. Additionally, it can be seen that the controlling model and the cost allocation method can be used independently from the sourcing option chosen.

The applicability of this method is strongly dependent on the interdependencies between the object to be sourced and other building blocks or services. If interdependencies exist as they have been pointed out when describing the sourcing examples, a further analysis of costs regarding their variability is needed. Variability of costs changes with the timeframe of a decision. The longer the planning period, the more fixed costs become variable costs, for instance, expiring contracts or ending depreciation of assets. In the short term, decisions can only affect variable costs.

In the past, many outsourcing decisions did not yield the cost reductions promised due to ignored interdependencies. The common example of replacing one building block service of an SAP system due to a more individual solution has already been mentioned. It is not necessarily true that total service costs can be saved by outsourcing a single service. In general, services share IT infrastructure assets like servers or the network, and in spite of termination of one service, other services keep using these assets. Problems like these will hopefully be reduced through modern technologies like hardware virtualization, which enable a more efficient use of resources through anticipating idle capacities.

6 Conclusion

6.1 Summary

Enterprise Architecture and SOA are complementary and they have to be used in conjunction to increase the flexibility of IT. When adopting SOA, economic operation and strategic controlling has to be ensured. IT controlling has been structured in IT supply and IT demand. Purposes, objectives, and tasks have been defined and special requirements in the given architectural environment have been shown. Additionally, it has been shown that the appropriate granularity of financial analyses has to be matched to a building block or a business service. This work introduces a policy-based controlling model that ensures consistent cost determination and cost allocation in order to allow for consistent financial calculations to support Enterprise Architecture Management. In practice, it has to be integrated with corporate controlling and value management.

To determine building block costs, CAPEX and OPEX have to be assessed throughout the life cycle. Investments can be CIO/CTO-driven or LOB-driven. CIO/CTO costs have to be shared by all LOBs in the group, whereas costs, emerging LOB-internal, are shared by corresponding building blocks. Costs are allocated bottom-up across the architectural layers on the basis of pricing policies. This allows to controlling the level of cost recovery. A different pricing policy may be chosen for each layer or actually for every single building block or service. Business service pricing includes determination of costs, usage planning, pricing, and enterprise-internal marketing. Business service prices, as the linkage between IT supply and IT demand, influence corporate performance and acceptance of controlling model application.

The implementation of the controlling model enables the application of controlling methods by providing the financial data needed. On the IT supply side, service portfolio optimization and building block portfolio optimization lead to improved IT provision. On the IT demand side, business service prices can be included in calculation of costs and results. The cost information gained about building blocks and services can also be used to support sourcing decisions and the examination of legacy systems. The hierarchical system of planning objects (domain, system, building block) shows different granularities of financial analyses, but it is equally useful to visualize controlling maturity and to support sourcing decisions and legacy system evaluations.

6.2 Model applicability

The developed controlling model has special characteristics which foster practical applicability and acceptance. The controlling model has been developed to control the Enterprise Architecture when adopting SOA. It does also support enterprises that are in the process of implementing SOA. In fact, there are many elements in this book that can also be used to control an Enterprise Architecture that has not adopted SOA. This is very important because SOA adoption, as well as SOA operation, is an evolutionary process. The freedom of choice regarding the preferred set of pricing policies creates potential for strategic controlling. It allows for evolutionary adoption and refinement of controlling, for instance, to start with cost-oriented transfer prices followed by a stepwise introduction of market-mechanisms.

The developed controlling model is based on Detecon's SOA layer model, but its application is not limited to this specific layer model. This has been shown by introducing the more general LANKES/MATTHES/WITTENBURG (2005) information model for Enterprise Architecture Management. The underlying approach of policy-based cost allocation across the architectural layers may also be transferred to any other order of building blocks. It is applicable for enterprises with different business backgrounds. It has been developed to allocate costs of IT provision to business units, which is the case in enterprise's that use IT to support their core business conducted in another domain, e.g. telecommunications, financial services, manufacturing, or process industries. The controlling model can also be applied for enterprises whose core business is IT. An Application Service Provider (ASP) offers services as products to the market. The controlling model can be used for costing, pricing, and performance evaluation of services. Additionally, the controlling model allows for application of favored controlling methods. The financial data provided enables optimization of IT supply and IT demand, and does not dictate to employ specific methods.

Summarizing, the developed controlling model offers a high level of freedom of choice, allowing for adoption to an enterprise's specific situation and requirements. There will be enterprises whose architecture is so different, that the controlling model gets inapplicable. But this work can also be helpful as a guideline to develop a suitable controlling model and a resource base to adopt single concepts and ideas.

6.3   Recommendations for further research

There are several possibilities for further research regarding controlling for Enterprise Architecture. However, there are two main areas particularly relevant for the developed controlling model:

- Reuse calculations:
  A method to measure the financial benefits of a reuse decision has to be developed. It has to consider cost savings through reuse of existing building blocks, but also additional expenses of change projects (generalization, adaptations, extension, etc.).

- Pricing policies:
  On the one hand, different pricing policies have to be evaluated regarding their appropriateness for different situations, for instance, how to refinance sponsoring. On the other hand, the benefits and drawbacks of introducing market-oriented transfer prices have to be analyzed. Additionally, IT governance has to define rules, responsibilities, and processes to regulate policy changes.

Appendix A: SOA layer model – UML class diagram

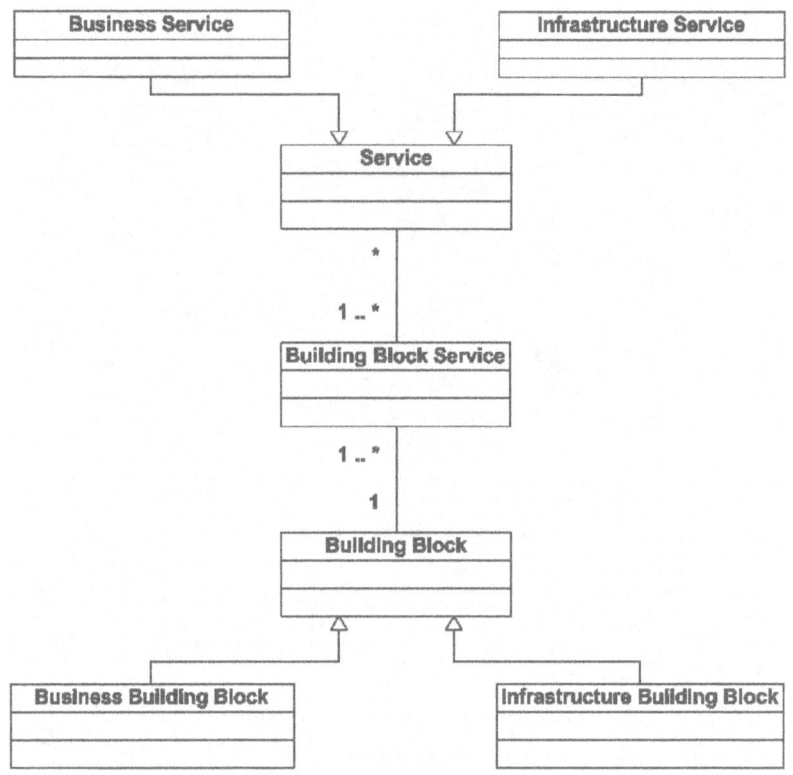

Bibliography

Aier/Dogan: Nachhaltigkeit 2004
Aier, S.; Dogan, T.: Nachhaltigkeit als Gestaltungsziel von Unternehmensarchitekturen, in: Aier, S.; Schönherr, M.: Enterprise Application Integration – Serviceorientierung und nachhaltige Architekturen, Berlin: GITO-Verlag 2004, page 75 - 124

Aier/Schönherr: EAI als Enabler 2004
Aier, S.; Schönherr, M.: Enterprise Application Integration als Enabler flexibler Unternehmensarchitekturen, in: Hasselbring, W.; Reichert, M.: EAI-Workshop 2004 - Enterprise Application Integration, Proceedings, Berlin: GITO-Verlag 2004, page 69 - 78

Arsanjani, Service-oriented modeling 2005
Arsanjani, A.: Service-oriented modeling and architecture, http://www-128.ibm.com/developerworks/webservices/library/ws-soa-design1/, [last visited 05.07.2006]

Berger/Lehner: Prozesskopplung 2002
Berger, S.; Lehner, F.: Intra- und interorganisationale Kooperation – Unterstützung der Prozesskopplung durch mobile Technologien, in: Bartmann, D. (publisher): Kopplung von Anwendungssystemen, FORWIN-Tagung 2002, Aachen: Shaker 2002

Bernard: Enterprise Architecture 2005
Bernard, S. A.: An introduction to Enterprise Architecture, 2nd edition, Bloomington: AuthorHouse 2005

Bieberstein et al.: SOA compass 2006
Bieberstein, N.; Bose, S.; Fiammante, M.; Jones, K.; Shah, R.: Service-oriented architecture compass: business value, planning and enterprise roadmap, IBM press, Upper Saddle River: Pearson 2006

Bradley: IT Costing 2003
Bradley, R.: Best Practices in IT Costing & Chargeback Solutions, 2003 http://www.crgroup.com/Downloads/PDFs/IT%20Cost_Chargeback%20Ron%20Bradley.pdf, [last visited 05.07.2006]

Braun: Prozeßkostenrechnung 1994
Braun, S.: Die Prozesskostenrechnung: Ein fortschrittliches Kostenrechnungssystem?, Ludwigsburg/Berlin: Wissenschaft & Praxis 1994

Burger: Kostenmanagement 1999
Burger, A: Kostenmanagement, 3rd edition, München: Oldenbourg 1999

Burkhard/Laures: SOA Paradigma 2003
    Burkhard, B.; Laures, G.: SOA – Wertstiftendes Architektur-Paradigma, in: Objektspektrum, issue 6, 2003, page 16 - 22, http://www.sigs.de/publications/os/2003/06/burkhard_OS_06_03.pdf, [last visited 05.07.2006]

Butler Group: Enterprise Architecture 2004
    Butler Group: Enterprise Architecture - An End-to-end Approach for Realigning IT with Business Aims, 2004

Capgemini: IT Trends 2006
    Capgemini: Studie IT-Trends 2006, http://www.de.capgemini.com/m/de/tl/IT-Trends_2006.pdf, [last visited 05.07.2006]

Carr: IT doesn't matter 2003
    Carr, N. G: IT Doesn't Matter, Harvard Business Review (HBR), volume 81, number 5, May 2003, page 41 - 49

Coenenberg: Kostenrechnung 2003
    Coenenberg, A. G.: Kostenrechnung und Kostenanalyse, 4th edition, Stuttgart: Schäffer-Poeschel 2003

Dearden: IS Organization 1987
    Dearden, J.: The Withering Away of the IS Organization, in: Sloan Management Review, volume 28, number 4, 1987, page 87 - 91

Detecon: Service Oriented Enterprise Architecture 2006
    Detecon: Service Oriented Enterprise Architecture, Sales Presentation, version 1.6, Mai 2006

Detecon: Strategic IT-Planning from Demand to Budget 2005
    Detecon: Strategic IT-Planning from Demand to Budget 2005, http://www.detecon.com/load.php?url=L211ZGlhL3BkZi9DYXNlX1N0dWR5X1RTSV8yU19lbmdsLnBkZg==, [last visited 05.07.2006]

Dittrich/Braun: Business Process Outsourcing 2004
    Dittrich, J.; Braun, M.: Business Process Outsourcing, Stuttgart: Schäffer-Poeschel 2004

Erl: Service-Oriented Architecture 2005
    Erl, T.: Service-Oriented Architecture – Concepts, Technology and Design, Upper Saddle River: Prentice Hall 2005

Ewert/Wagenhofer: Interne Unternehmensrechnung 2005
    Ewert, R.; Wagenhofer, A.: Interne Unternehmensrechnung, 6th edition, Berlin: Springer 2005

Fernholz/Kielwein/Buresch: IV-Produkt-Controlling 2000
Fernholz, M.; Kielwein, L.; Buresch, A.: IV-Produkt-Controlling –
Lebenszyklusorientes Systemmanagement bei Outsourcing, in: Krcmar, H.;
Buresch, A.; Reb, M. (publisher): IV-Controlling auf dem Prüfstand,
Wiesbaden: Gabler 2000, page 57 - 74

Figueiredo/Dinda/Fortes: Virtualization 2005
Figueiredo, R.; Dinda, P. A.; Fortes, J.: Resource Virtualization Renaissance,
Computer Magazin, May 2005, page 28 – 31,
http://csdl2.computer.org/comp/mags/co/2005/05/r5028.pdf,
[last visited 05.07.2006]

Fischer: Kostencontrolling 2000
Fischer, T. M.: Kosten-Controlling: neue Methoden und Inhalte, Stuttgart:
Schäffer-Poeschel 2000

Forrester Research: Enterprise Architecture of SOA 2006
Forrester Research: Enterprise Architecture of SOA 2006

Forrester Research: IT Governance 2005
Forrester Research: IT Governance Framework - Structures, Processes, and
Communication, 2005

Forrester Research: Time for SOA 2006
Forrester Research: Survey Data Says: The Time For SOA Is Now, 2006

Frankel et al.: Zachman and MDA 2003
Frankel, D. S.; Harmon, P. Mukerji, J.; Odell, J.; Owen, M.; Rivitt, P.; Rosen,
M.; Soley, R. M.: The Zachman Framework and the OMG's Model Driven
Architecture, 2003,
http://www.omg.org/mda/mda_files/09-03-WP_Mapping_MDA_to_Zachman_F
ramework1.pdf,
[last visited 05.07.2006]

Gadatsch: IT-Controlling 2005
Gadatsch, A.: IT-Controlling realisieren, Wiesbaden: Vieweg 2005

Gadatsch/Mayer: IT-Controlling 2004
Gadatsch, A.; Mayer, E.: Grundkurs IT-Controlling, Wiesbaden: Vieweg 2004

Gallas/Schönherr: Service Management 2005
Gallas, B. E.; Schönherr, M.: Service Management als Grundlage Service
Orientierter Architekturen – Ein SOA-Testszenario, in: Aier, S.; Schönherr, M.
(publisher): Unternehmensarchitekturen und Systemintegration, Berlin: GITO-
Verlag 2005, page 221 - 245

Gartner: Outsourcing 2005
Gartner: Gartner on Outsourcing, 2005

Gerick: IT-Controlling 2003
    Gerick, T.: IT-Controlling – Brücke zwischen Betriebswirtschaft und
    Informationstechnologie, 2003,
    http://www.competence-site.de/itmanagement.nsf/21D9795FAC0AB0F4C1256
    DC10045FDB5/$File/it-controlling_br%FCcke_zwischen_bwl_und_it.pdf,
    [last visited 05.07.2006]

Granof/Platt/Vaysman: Activity-Based Costing 2000
    Granof, M. H.; Platt, D. H.; Vaysman, I.: Using Activity-Based Costing to
    Manage More Effectively, 2000,
    http://www.businessofgovernment.org/pdfs/GranofReport.pdf,
    [last visited 05.07.2006]

Groves: Planning SOA 2005
    Groves, D.: Successfully Planning for SOA, 2005,
    http://dev2dev.bea.com/pub/a/2005/11/planning-for-soa.html,
    [last visited 05.07.2006]

Hafner/Schelp/Winter: Architekturmanagement 2004
    Hafner, M.; Schelp, J.; Winter, R.: Architekturmanagement als Basis effizienter
    und effektiver Produktion von IT-Services, in: Meier, A.; Myrach, T.
    (publisher): IT-Servicemanagement, Praxis der Wirtschaftsinformatik,
    HMD 237, 2004, page 54 - 66

Hauer/Settele: IV-Controlling durch Outsourcing 2000
    Hauer, G.; Settle, B.: IV-Controlling durch Outsourcing?, in: Krcmar, H.;
    Buresch, A.; Reb, M. (publisher): IV-Controlling auf dem Prüfstand,
    Wiesbaden: Gabler 2000, page 171 - 187

Hardt/Rindler: Wertorientierte Unternehmensführung 2003
    Hardt, F.-S.; Rindler, G.: Wertorientierte Unternehmensführung in einem
    IT/TK-Unternehmen, in: Zeitschrift für Controlling und Management (ZfCM),
    volume 47, issue 4, 2003, page 273 - 277

Harrison/Varveris: Establishing TOGAF 2004
    Harrison, D.; Varveris, L.: TOGAF: Establishing Itself As the Definitive Method
    for Building Enterprise Architectures in the Commercial World, 2004,
    www.developer.com/design/article.php/3374171,
    [last visited 05.07.2006]

Heinen/Dietel Kostenrechnung 1991
    Heinen, E.; Dietel, B.: Kostenrechnung, in: Heinen, E. (publisher):
    Industriebetriebslehre: Entscheidungen im Industriebetrieb, 9th edition,
    Wiesbaden: Gabler 1991, page 1157 – 1313

Hirnle/Hess: IT-Investitionsentscheidungen 2004
    Hirnle, C.; Hess, T.: Rationale IT-Investitionsentscheidungen: Hürden und
    Hilfsmittel, in: Controlling & Management, special edition 1, 2004, page 86 - 95

Hodel/Berger/Risi: Outsourcing 2004
    Hodel, M.; Berger, A.; Risi, P.: Outsourcing realisieren, Wiesbaden: Vieweg
    2004

Horváth: Controlling 2004
Horvath, P.: Controlling, 9. Auflage, München: Vahlen 2004

Horváth: Strategiekompetenz 2000
Horvath, P.: Strategiekompetenz und Umsetzungskompetenz verbinden, in: Foschiani, S.; Habenicht, W.; Schmid, U.; Wäscher, G. (publisher): Strategisches Management im Zeichen von Umbruch und Wandel, Stuttgart: Schäffer-Poeschel 2000, page 77 - 93

Horváth/Rieg: strategisches IT-Controlling 2001
Horváth, P.; Rieg, R.: Grundlagen des strategischen IT-Controllings, in: Heilmann, H. (publisher): Strategisches IT-Controlling, Praxis der Wirtschaftsinformatik, HMD 217, 2001, page 9 - 18

Hurwitz: Industrialization 2005
Hurwitz, J.: SOA – Towards the Industrialization of Software, CIO online, Analyst Corner, August 22nd 2005,
http://www2.cio.com/analyst/report3817.html,
[last visited 05.07.2006]

Institute of Electrical and Electronics Engineers: ANSI/IEEE Std 1471-2000 2000
Institute of Electrical and Electronics Engineers: ANSI/IEEE Std 1471-2000: ANSI/IEEE Std 1471-2000 IEEE Recommended Practice for Architectural Description of Software-Intensive Systems, 2000

International Group of Controlling: Mission Statement 2001
International Group of Controlling: Mission Statement 2001,
http://www.igc-controlling.org/engl/mission/mission.html,
[last visited 05.07.2006]

IT Governance Institute: Board Briefing 2003
IT Governance Institute (ITGI): Board Briefing on IT Governance, 2nd Edition, 2003
http://www.isaca.org/Content/ContentGroups/ITGI3/Resources1/Board_Briefing _on_IT_Governance/26904_Board_Briefing_final.pdf,
[last visited 05.07.2006]

Kargl: Controlling 1996
Kargl, H.: Controlling im DV-Bereich, 3. Auflage, München: Oldenbourg 1996

Kaplan/Atkinson: Advanced Management Accounting 1998
Kaplan, R. S.; Atkinson, A. A.: Advanced Management Accounting, 3rd edition, Upper Saddle River: Prentice Hall 1998

Keller/Nüttgens/Scheer: EPK Modellierung 1992
Keller, G.; Nüttgens, M.; Scheer, A.-W.: Semantische Prozessmodellierung auf der Grundlage Ereignisgesteuerter Prozeßketten (EPK), in: Scheer, A.-W. (publisher): Veröffentlichungen des Instituts für Wirtschaftsinformatik (IWi), Universität des Saarlandes, Heft 89, Januar 1992,
http://www.iwi.uni-sb.de/Download/iwihefte/heft89.pdf,
[last visited 05.07.2006]

Koslowski/Kohlmeier: Controlling Wörterbuch 2001
Koslowski, F.; Kohlmeier, U.: Controlling-Wörterbuch der Praxis, Stuttgart: Lucius & Lucius 2001

Krafzig/Banke/Slama: Enterprise SOA 2005
Krafzig, D.; Banke, K.; Slama, D.: Enterprise SOA – Service-Oriented Architecture Best Practices, Upper Saddle River: Pearson 2005

Krcmar: Informationsmanagement 2005
Krcmar, H.: Informationsmanagement, 4th edition, Berlin: Springer 2005

Kütz: IT Controlling 2005
Kütz, M.: IT Controlling für die Praxis 2005, Heidelberg: dpunkt 2005

Kütz: Kennzahlen der IT 2003
Kütz, M.: Kennzahlen in der IT – Werkzeuge für Controlling und Management, Heidelberg: dpunkt 2003

Lankes/Matthes/Wittenburg: Architekturmanagement 2005
Lankes, J.; Matthes, F.; Wittenburg, A.: Softwarekartographie als Beitrag zum Architekturmanagement, in: Aier, S.; Schönherr, M. (publisher): Unternehmensarchitekturen und Systemintegration, Berlin: GITO-Verlag 2005, page 305 - 330

Lankhorst et al.: Enterprise Architecture 2005
Lankhorst, M. et al.: Enterprise Architecture at Work, Berlin: Springer 2005

Masak: Enterprise Architekturen 2005
Masak, D.: Moderne Enterprise Architekturen, Berlin: Springer 2005

Michels: IT-Betriebsabrechnung 2004
Michels, J. K.: IT-Betriebsabrechnung. Der BAB des Rechenzentrums, Neuss: VDM 2004

Michels/Pölzl: CIO 2002
Michels, M.; Pölzl, J.: Der CIO – Verwalter oder Gestalter, http://www.de.capgemini.com/m/de/tl/Der_CIO_-_Verwalter_oder_Gestalter_.pdf,
[last visited 05.07.2006]

Miller/Vollmann: The Hidden factory 1985
Miller, J. G.; Vollmann, Th. E.: The hidden factory, in: Harvard Business Review, volume 63, 1985, page 142 - 150

Mintzberg/Westley: Decision Making 2001
Mintzberg, H.; Westley, F.: Decision Making: It's not what you think, in: MIT Sloan Management Review, volume 42, issue 3, 2001, page 89 - 94

Morgenthal: The A in SOA 2006
Morgenthal, J. P.: Enterprise Architecture: The Holistic View: The A in SOA is Architecture, DM Review Online, 2006, http://www.dmreview.com/article_sub.cfm?articleId=1046478,
[last visited 05.07.2006]

Natis: Service Oriented Architecture 2004
    Natis, Y. V.: Service-oriented Architecture (SOA) ushers in the next era in business software engineering, in: Business Integration Journal, number 5, 2004, page 23 - 25

Niemann: Unternehmensarchitektur 2005
    Niemann, K. D.: Von der Unternehmensarchitektur zur IT-Governance, Wiesbaden: Vieweg 2005

Niessen/Oldenburg: Service Level Management 1997
    Niessen, J.; Oldenburg, P.: Service Level Management: Customer Focused, London: The Stationery Office Books 1997

Oey/Wagner/Rehbach/Bachmann: Serviceorientierte Architekturen 2005
    Oey, K. J.; Wagner, H; Rehbach, S.; Bachmann, A.: Mehr als alter Wein in neuen Schläuchen: Eine einführende Darstellung des Konzepts der serviceorientierte Architekturen, in: Aier, S.; Schönherr, M. (publisher): Unternehmensarchitekturen und Systemintegration, Berlin: GITO-Verlag 2005

Organization for Economic Cooperation and Development: Corporate Governance 2004
    Organization for Economic Cooperation and Development (OECD): Principles of Corporate Governance, 2004,
    http://www.oecd.org/dataoecd/32/18/31557724.pdf,
    [last visited 05.07.2006]

Porter/Millar: Competitive Advantage 1985
    Porter, M. E.; Millar, V. E.: How information gives you Competitive Advantage, in: Harvard Business Review, volume 63, issue 4, 1985, page 149 - 160

Pulier/Taylor: Enterprise SOA 2006
    Pulier, E.; Taylor, H.: Understanding Enterprise SOA, Greenwich: Manning Publications 2006

Ross/Rockart: Reconceptualizing IT 1999
    Ross, J. W.; Rockart, J. F.: Reconceptualizing IT, Center for Information Systems Research (CISR) Working Paper 302, 1999,
    http://web.mit.edu/cisr/working%20papers/cisrwp302.pdf,
    [last visited 05.07.2006]

Ross/Vitale/Beath: IT chargeback 1999
    Ross, J. W.; Vitale, M. R.; Beath, C. M.: The untapped potential of IT chargeback, MIS quarterly, volume 23, issue 2, 1999,
    http://misbridge.mccombs.utexas.edu/knowledge/facpubs/articles/chargeback.doc,
    [last visited 05.07.2006]

SAP: NetWeaver 2005
    SAP: NetWeaver – Solution Overview, 2005,
    http://www.sap.com/platform/netweaver/pdf/BW_OV_SAP_NetWeaver_Solution_Overview.pdf,
    [last visited 05.07.2006]

Schekkerman: Enterprise Architecture 2005
   Schekkerman, J.: The Economic Benefits of Enterprise Architecture, Victoria: Trafford Publishing 2005

Schekkerman: Service Oriented Architecture 2006
   Schekkerman, J.: Service Oriented Architecture 2006,
   http://www.enterprise-architecture.info/Images/Services%20Oriented%20Enterprise/EA_Service-Oriented-Architecture1.htm,
   [last visited 05.07.2006]

Schmale: Real-Time Enterprise 2004
   Schmale, T.: Mit EAI und SOA zum Real-Time Enterprise,
   http://www.competence-site.de/gpm.nsf/E59B19C7AF5A64C4C1256E68003348CB/$File/real-time_enterprise_0304.pdf,
   [last visited 05.07.2006]

Schmelzer: ROI of SOA 2006
   Schmelzer, R.: ROI of SOA, 10.02.2006,
   http://www.zapthink.com/report.html?id=ZTZN-1187,
   [last visited 05.07.2006]

Schweitzer/Küpper: Kosten- und Erlösrechnung 2003
   Schweitzer, M.; Küpper, H.-U.: Systeme der Kosten- und Erlösrechnung, 8th edition, München: Vahlen 2003

Sebis: EA Tool Survey 2005
   Lehrstuhl für Software Engineering betrieblicher Informationssysteme (sebis) TU München: Enterprise Architecture Management Tool Survey 2005

TechConsult/Lünendonk: Outsourcing Services 2004
   TechConsult GmbH und Lünendonk GmbH: Outsourcing Services Deutschland 2004 - 2006, 2004

The Open Group: Building Blocks and the ADM 1998
   The Open Group: Building Blocks and the ADM,
   http://www.opengroup.org/public/arch/p4/bbs/bbs_adm.htm,
   [last visited 05.07.2006]

The Open Group: Introduction to Building Blocks 1999
   The Open Group: Introduction to Building Blocks,
   http://www.opengroup.org/architecture/togaf8-doc/arch/p4/bbs/bbs_intro.htm,
   [last visited 05.07.2006]

The Open Group: TOGAF 8.1 2004
   The Open Group: TOGAF 8.1 2004,
   http://www.opengroup.org/architecture/togaf8-doc/arch/,
   [last visited 05.07.2006]

The Open Group: TOGAF FAQ 2002
   TOGAF Frequently Asked Questions, 2002,
   http://www.opengroup.org/architecture/togaf8-doc/arch/p1/togaf_faq.htm,
   [last visited 05.07.2006]

Bibliography

The Open Group: TOGAF website 2006
www.opengroup.org/architecture/togaf,
[last visited 05.07.2006]

The Open Group: TOGAF Zachman mapping 2002
The Open Group: Mapping the TOGAF ADM to the Zachman Framework,
2002,
http://www.opengroup.org/architecture/togaf8-doc/arch/p4/zf/zf_mapping.htm
[last visited 05.07.2006]

Voß/Gutenschwager: Informationsmanagement 2001
Voß, S.; Gutenschwager, K.: Informationsmanagement, Berlin: Springer 2001

Weber: Business Enabling Architecture 2002
Weber, U.: Business Enabling Architecture - Die Methode für eine integrierte
Geschäftsabwicklung, in: Detecon Management Report (DMR) 08/2002,
page 6 - 8,
http://www.detecon.com/load.php?url=L21lZGlhL3BkZi9ETVJfMDhfMDJfR2
VzY2hhZWZ0c2Fid2lja2wucGRm,
[last visited 05.07.2006]

Weber/Schmidtmann: Concurrent Planning 2006
Weber, U; Schmidtmann, V.: Concurrent Planning - Als Business Partner
gemeinsam planen, in: Detecon Management Report (DMR) 02/2006,
page 29 - 33,
http://www.detecon.com/load.php?url=L21lZGlhL3BkZi9ETVJfMDFfMDZfQ2
9uY3VycmVudFBsYW5uaW5nX2R0LnBkZg==,
[last visited 05.07.2006]

Weill/Ross: IT Governance 2004
Weill, P.; Ross, J. W.: IT Governance, Boston: Harvard Business School Press
2004

Wiemers et al.: Entscheidungsfall Vorgehensmodell 2005
Wiemers, M. et al.: Entscheidungsfall Vorgehensmodell, 12. Workshop der
Fachgruppe WI-VM "Entscheidungsfall Vorgehensmodell" der Gesellschaft für
Informatik e.V. 2005,
http://www.kbst.bund.de/cln_011/SharedDocs/Anlagen-kbst/V-Modell/V-Model
l-Publikationen-Anlagen/wi-vm05-band-pdf,templateId=raw,property=publicati
onFile.pdf/wi-vm05-band-pdf.pdf,
[last visited 05.07.2006]

Wiggers et al.: IT Performance Management 2004
Wiggers, P.; de Boer-de Wit, M.; Kok, H.: IT Performance Management,
Burlington: Butterworth-Heinemann 2004

Wöhe: Allgemeine Betriebswitschaftslehre 2002
Wöhe, G.: Einführung in die Allgemeine Betriebswitschaftslehre, 21st edition,
München: Vahlen 2002

Woods: Enterprise Services Architecture 2004
Woods, D.: Enterprise Services Architecture, Bonn: Galileo Press 2004

Zachman: Enterprise Architecture Framework 2001
Zachman, J. A.: Enterprise Architecture Framework 2001,
http://www.zifa.com/framework.pdf,
[last visited 05.07.2006]

Zachman: Extending the Framework 1992
Zachman, J. A.: Extending and formalizing the framework for information systems architecture, IBM Systems Journal, volume 31, number 3, 1992,
http://www.research.ibm.com/journal/sj/313/sowa.pdf,
[last visited 05.07.2006]

Zachman: Framework for Information Systems Architecture 1987
Zachman, J. A.: Framework for Information Systems Architecture, IBM Systems Journal, volume 26, number 3, 1987,
http://www.research.ibm.com/journal/sj/263/ibmsj2603E.pdf,
[last visited 05.07.2006]

Zachman: The challenge is change 1996
Zachman, J. A.: The challenge is change, 1996,
http://www.ies.aust.com/~visible/papers/zachman2.htm,
[last visited 05.07.2006]

Zachman Institute for Framework Advancement: website 2006
www.zifa.com,
[last visited 05.07.2006]

Zarnekow/Brenner: Kosten im Lebenszyklus 2004
Zarnekow, R.; Brenner, W.: Einmalige und wiederkehrende Kosten im Lebenszyklus von IT-Anwendungen – Eine empirische Untersuchung, in: Zeitschrift für Controlling und Management (ZfCM), volume 48, issue 5, 2004, page 336 – 339